Judge Dave

and the

Rainbow People

David B. Sentelle

GREEN BAG PRESS
WASHINGTON DC
2002

GREEN BAG PRESS
6600 Barnaby Street NW
Washington, DC 20015

Green Bag Press is a division of
The Green Bag, Inc., publisher of
*The Green Bag, Second Series,
an Entertaining Journal of Law.*
"The Green Bag" and associated logos
are our registered trademarks.

For more information, please email
editors@greenbag.org or visit
http://www.greenbag.org.

Portions of this book previously appeared in
volume 3 of the *Green Bag*.

Proceeds from sales of this book will be
donated to the Oliver Wendell Holmes
Devise Fund, to support the continued
publication of its *History of the Supreme
Court of the United States.* The author has
refused any compensation.

Thanks to the Foundation for Research on
Economics and the Environment, Gallatin
Writers, and William J. Kilberg and his
partners in the DC office of Gibson, Dunn &
Crutcher LLP for supporting this project.

This book was
designed by Montgomery Kosma
in Annandale, Virginia, and
printed by Joe Christensen, Inc.,
in Lincoln, Nebraska.

Its typefaces include Adobe
Caflisch Script Pro and Warnock Pro,
both designed by Robert Slimbach.

Artwork courtesy of Amy Davies
(NC & campground maps, and cover &
chapter-end icons except for the Rainbow
and flying heart) and the Rainbow Archives
(everything else).

Front cover photographs courtesy of
David Sentelle (Judge Dave); Garrick
Beck (troopers & kid; crowd background);
W.D.N.C. (Asheville Federal Courthouse);
and Bob Scott (everything else).

Rear cover photographs courtesy of Melanie
Morris James (herself); Garrick Beck
(troopers; Road Closed); College Park Press,
http://www.cgpp.com/bookland (bar code);
and Bob Scott (everything else).

Inside photographs courtesy of Garrick
Beck (pages 263, 266, & 269) and Bob Scott
(everything else).

*ISBN 0-9677568-3-9,
Library of Congress Control No. 2002107516.*

I wish to acknowledge the contributions to this
book by Monty Kosma, without whom it would
still be gathering dust in my desk drawer;
Ross Davies, without whom it might never
have been published; and especially
Melanie Morris James, without whom
a lot of the incidents described herein
would never have occurred, or at least
would have been a lot less fun.

— DBS

Contents

Preface xi   John A. Baden & Ramona Marotz-Baden

Introduction xvii   C. Boyden Gray

Prologue 1

Part I Toward World Peace & Healing 3

1 * IGNORANCE IS BLISS 4

2 * THE BEGINNING OF WISDOM 11

3 * YOU'LL NEVER BELIEVE THE VIEW 20

Part II In the Camp of the Rainbows 29

4 * WELCOME HOME 30

5 * OF BUMPERS & BABIES, KITCHENS & CAMPS 39

6 * OF HIPPIES, HOLLOWS & HOLES 48

7 * ON "CALM – MASH" &
        NOT-SO-CALM OBSERVERS 53

8 * WHO ARE THE RAINBOWS? 61

9 * ON BARTER, BABIES & WHY RAINBOWS
        ARE NOT REALLY MULTI-COLORED 70

10 * MORE ON HEALTH, HIPPIE CLOTHES &
        HANDSOME HIKERS 79

11 ✦ ON A SYMBOLIC SHOWER CURTAIN &
A PLEASANT PACHYDERM   87

12 ✦ ENTERTAINMENT, REST & RELAXATION
(OF BODY & RULES)   93

13 ✦ BACK TOWARD NORMALCY   97

14 ✦ DOWN & OUT   101

Part III Toward a Day of Decision   107

15 ✦ A LESSON IN THE LAW –
THEORY OR PRACTICE?   108

16 ✦ A HARD DAY'S NIGHT   113

17 ✦ A-COURTING WE WILL GO   116

18 ✦ STATE V. THE HIPPIES   133

19 ✦ THE AGE OF CONSENT   140

20 ✦ JUST (OR UNJUST?) FOR THE RECORD   150

Part IV Return to the Rainbows   159

21 ✦ THE RATIO AT THE BRIDGE   160

22 ✦ IT AIN'T OVER WHEN IT'S OVER   167

23 ✦ ON THE TRAIL AGAIN   186

24 ✦ STAND FOR THE BENEDICTION   193

25 ✦ MURPHY'S LAW & ORDER   196

26 ✦ THE EYES & EARS OF THE FOREST   200

Part V Looking for the End
of the Rainbows 205

27 ✦ DON'T KILL ALL THE LAWYERS 206

28 ✦ WHO SHALL THE GUARDIANS GUARD? 214

29 ✦ MERRILY THEY ROLL THEIR OWN 224

30 ✦ FREE THE RAINBOW EIGHT 237

Epilogue 243

Garrick Beck's Reflections on Judge Dave 245

1 ✦ TO CRACK THE NUT, YOU ONLY HAVE TO
CRACK THE NUTSHELL 246

2 ✦ A FEW WORDS ABOUT MYSELF 252

3 ✦ ONE RALPH, TWO RALPHS, RUSSIAN BOARS &
RUMORS GALORE 254

4 ✦ OUR DAYS IN COURT 257

5 ✦ VIDEO VILLAINY? 262

6 ✦ IN THE JUDGE'S CHAMBERS 266

7 ✦ AND IN THE END 267

Preface

David Sentelle was a federal district judge in North Carolina prior to his elevation to the U.S. Court of Appeals for the D.C. Circuit. During the Senate confirmation hearings in 1987 he had a remarkably difficult, indeed bizarre, case in process. It featured conflicts among liberty, ecology, cultures, and jurisdictions.

The specific conflict involved state rules governing public health versus constitutional rights of the Rainbow Family to assembly in a national forest. This situation conjoined a large set of environmental and cultural disagreements. We are fortunate indeed that a person of Judge Dave's character, temperament, and intelligence heard and settled this case, for there were no easy or obvious answers. Here's why.

Environmental problems normally share two features. First, they are technically or scientifically complex. Second, they carry heavy emotional baggage. These ingredients foster error, acrimony, and opportunistic behavior.

Environmental issues usually fall into one of two categories: romance or sludge. The romantic involve natural features and creatures, *e.g.*, wilderness areas, forests, or habitat for charismatic animals like the gray wolf. Sludge issues are usually far more important in terms of human health and well-being but they are less dramatic and picturesque.

Seldom do environmental conflicts involve romance

and sludge issues plus fundamental constitutional rights, in this case the right to peacefully assemble absent the imprimatur of the North Carolina State Department of Health. This book is a story of, and a testimony to, the ability of a judge to balance these contentious matters.

My wife Ramona and I have a perspective on this story which has been broadened by our experiences with both the judge and the Rainbow Family, who unofficially describe themselves as "the largest non-organization of non-members in the world" who are "into intentional community building, non-violence, and alternative lifestyles." A decade after his ruling, we had the great good fortune to host Judge Dave at one of our week-long seminars for federal judges that explore potentials to harmonize environmental concerns with economic and cultural realities. It was held at an old guest ranch nestled in a national forest adjacent to the one the Rainbow Family later selected for their gathering in 2000. Strictly by accident Ramona and I were intimately involved with this Rainbow gathering.

Ramona, a professor at Montana State, was studying the accommodation of multigenerational ranch families to fundamental change in their economic, political, and cultural environment. Her study site was the Big Hole Valley of Beaverhead County, Montana. This is one of America's largest, most remote, and most conservative counties. Although larger than Connecticut, its population is less than 10,000.

Because we ranch several hours east of the Big Hole, we leased the only apartment available in Jackson, Montana, population 47. From there, Ramona conducted her interviews. One of her primary sources was Harold Peterson, a highly respected third-generation rancher, community leader, and conservationist.

The federal government owns roughly half of the land west of the 100th meridian. In Beaverhead County it's nearly 60%. The valley floors were homesteaded a century ago. Ranchers run their cows on Forest Service and Bureau of Land Management land in the summer and raise hay and winter their stock in the valley. Most ranchers have an assigned allotment on a specific area of the forest. They "turn out" their stock on a designated date.

But in the summer of 2000, 23,000 members of the Rainbow Family drifted into the Beaverhead National Forest. Their huge camp gradually expanded into the corrals and loading chutes and part of Peterson's allotment just before the Petersons were to turn out their stock. It would be difficult to conjure a more extreme clash of cultures. But both groups adjusted. Peterson waited over ten days, until he was out of feed, to move in cattle, and the Rainbows finally moved their makeshift dwellings, colorfully festooned VW vans, and assorted paraphernalia. Each was shooting photos of the other as the semi trucks unloaded cattle into the corrals recently cleared of Rainbows by Forest Service personnel.

A few weeks later, after most Rainbows had drifted out of the forest, we were eating in the Jackson Hot Springs Lodge, across from our apartment. It was clear that leaders of this "leaderless" group were meeting at the adjacent table. We asked to join them, to discuss how they dealt with constraints imposed by the local law enforcement and Forest Service personnel. We had spoken with a number of sheriff's deputies and members of the Forest Service's Strategic Management teams and had watched some drug busts. "Welcome Woman," a.k.a. Joanee Freedom, enthusiastically told us about Judge Dave and his 1987 rulings in North Carolina. When we told them we knew Judge Dave they smiled and willingly shared their experiences.

This book is not about the summer when we met the Rainbows, but rather that of 1987. Yet, the earlier decisions of Judge Dave set governing precedents. While conflicts of rights and responsibilities, legal and ecological, are inevitable whenever 20-odd-thousand hippies, new agers, and assorted camp followers descend on an isolated rural area, his decision seems to minimize damages and foster accommodations.

We urge you to read this book − but when you

select your reading site be as careful as the Rainbows are in picking annual meeting sites. It's likely that you will be unable to contain your laughter and will be sorely tempted to share passages with those around you.

Welcome home.

John A. Baden & Ramona Marotz-Baden
F.R.E.E. / Gallatin Writers
Bozeman, Montana
May 2002

WELCOME HOME!

Introduction

In writing an introduction to Judge David Sentelle's book, titled *Judge Dave and the Rainbow People*, I have significant conflicts of interest: I was a law school classmate of David's at the UNC Law School, I am a native of North Carolina who spent a lot of time in the summers in the mountains not far from the locus of this book, and I practice mostly administrative law which is greatly affected by the court where David sits. I might therefore be expected to give a good review, whatever I really thought.

Well, let me tell you. This is a priceless gem of a book, a must-read for anyone who lived through the '60s and the '70s, who would like to know what hippies are all about, who is interested in the law, or who would like to be greatly amused for 250 pages or so.

It is, of course, especially amusing if you know David Sentelle.

But first, a little of the context.

The story is about a bunch of largely, but not exclusively, middle-aged hippies who want to have their annual camp-out meeting at a National Park in the beautiful mountains of Western North Carolina. State and federal officials believe the hippies are in violation of the applicable law controlling the size of campsites. The hippies, on the other hand, believe the controlling law violates their rights of free speech.

The many legal questions that come to mind quickly land on the desk of Judge David Sentelle, a federal District Court judge just recently nominated by President Reagan to the D.C. Circuit. What law applies, federal or state; does a federal judge have jurisdiction; is the North Carolina law, which strictly construed may not permit the gathering, subject to being ruled unconstitutional by a federal judge; and even if it is, is David Sentelle such a judge, considering that he grew up in the area, is a conservative Republican and is, at the time the crisis erupts, hoping to get confirmed by the Democratic Senate to the Court of Appeals for the D.C. Circuit. And why cannot Judge Dave, as the hippies came to call him, duck this whole thing anyway and ship it down to the local courts?

In this delightful book, Judge Dave runs through the legal issues in a way that can be easily understood by the layman, and then basically sidesteps them altogether. For me, this is the most instructive part of the book, because of the obvious tension between the need to observe the rule of law and the need to maintain peace and tranquility, sometimes otherwise known as common sense.

So Judge Dave consults his deceased predecessor on the bench, known as "Coot." (This consultation might scare some people, especially people who have cases before Judge Dave, but let me reassure you that his willingness to consult the dead is most reassuring, if you know Judge Dave.)

"Sentelle," [Coot] would have said, "what those hippies want is to have their party. What the State of North Carolina wants to do is look after the Tapoco watershed and try to keep those hippies from making any more folks sick around the camp than what's gonna get sick anyway. Now you just forget 'bout all your high falutin' theories for a minute and take the common sense that God gave you back into chambers with those two lawyers and beat their heads together 'til they consent to something that accomplishes all those goals."

And as the Judge says, "That was just about what I did."

The book is a masterpiece of storytelling about how Judge Dave accomplished his goal without compromising either his principles or the rule of law. But you won't get the point if you don't have a sense of humor. At the same time, it is impossible to read the book and not laugh, thus learning a sense of humor if you did not have one starting out.

For one thing, Judge Dave tells the reader what happens when one eats ramps, a mountain delicacy related to onions and garlic, with some of the same consequences. Thus, Judge Dave informs us what it's like being in chambers with "ramp-eating, herb-smoking, shower-dodging hippies" who have been in the woods for a while: "the odor is somewhere between that of a sweating mare trampling through a field of garlic, and a wet dog smoking a cheap cigar."

He also informs the reader of something every hiker in the Blue Ridge or Shenandoah should know about drinking spring water in the mountains, which is something you might think would be one of the reasons you would want to spend a couple of weeks in the mountains. Well, be careful – a message that had to be communicated to the Rainbow People. The problem, at least where they were camped out, was that the area was inhabited by wild hogs imported during the 19th century by wealthy sportsmen for hunting purposes without understanding what the hogs would do to the ecology. "Their habit is to make wallows of any open spring they find," Judge Dave writes. "As it happens, these swine are commonly host to shigellæ," which causes dysentery, he notes.

This observation led Judge Dave inevitably to want to see some of their latrines. "Actually," he writes, " I did not want to see any of the latrines, but I felt I should." What he discovered, among other things, was a material difference between what the Rainbow People were doing and what the Marine Corps Manual recommends. "The Marine literature recommends screening the latrine with canvas. Rainbows do not screen their latrines with anything," he writes. You have to read the book to discover the consequences of this discrepancy. Suffice it here to quote the Judge:

> There are certain necessary functions which are not like justice. We say in the law that justice should not only be done, it should be seen to be done. Certain functions which must be done should not be seen to be done.

You get the picture. One thing was clear to me about David when we shared offices on the *Law Review* at UNC and that was that he was very down-to-earth and totally without pretense. When you read the book you realize how little he has been corrupted by his very considerable success. In fact, I believe he very much enjoyed managing this hippie reunion and would have found a way to work it into his schedule – and not try to get out of the case or shut the reunion down – regardless of what "Coot" advised him. And he makes it quite clear that at least one of his two female law clerks was quite sad when the reunion ended of its own accord and everyone went home.

I do not believe that he was influenced in any way by his pending nomination. When he informed an old friend one day that he had spent the day at a "mass hippie gathering," there was a long pause and the friend replied, "I know you want to seek favor with the liberals, Sentelle, but this is ridiculous." Of course, David would have been confirmed anyway. But the book speaks for itself as to the nature of the experience and how much, despite himself, David enjoyed it.

And any reader will enjoy it. The book is both edifying and highly amusing. It is hard to put down. The only problem with it is that it eventually comes to an end.

C. Boyden Gray
Washington, D.C.
May 2002

Judge Dave

and the

Rainbow People

Prologue

Hippies are not extinct. I am not sure that they are even an endangered species. This is the story of how 15,000 of them came together in the back woods of Western North Carolina – in an area peopled by conservatives, farmers, rednecks, and Reagan-appointed judges.

Like the ballad of Frankie and Johnnie "this story has no moral," and further like that ballad, "this story has no end," at least in the sense that "end" implies some punch line or conclusion. What this story does have going for it is the fact that it is true, that it is shot with irony, and that it was brought to my mind by two apparently unrelated occurrences: the first being the failed nomination to the Supreme Court of my friend and former colleague Robert Bork, the second being a request for time off by one of my law clerks.

More on the law clerk later. We turn first to the failed fight for the confirmation of Brother Bork. During that battle, many of his supporters, my fellow conservatives, renewed their expression of our concerns about activist liberal judges who overstep their proper bounds of office and try to be legislators and executives. All of my career, not only as a judge but as a lawyer and law student, I've fretted about the extended power of the judge who takes over and operates a prison, a school system, or a housing authority. That's why it becomes especially ironic that I am, so far as I know, the only federal judge who took over and operated a hippie reunion.

Part I

Toward World Peace
& Healing

1 ⚭ IGNORANCE IS BLISS

The reunion in question officially occurred in July of 1987 in a remote area of the mountains of Western North Carolina in a section of the Nantahala National Forest near the little town of Tapoco, North Carolina, which in turn is near Robbinsville, the county seat of Graham County, North Carolina, which in turn is not near anything but the ground – the ground and some of the most beautiful mountains, lakes, streams, and other acts of God and nature to be found in these United States. That, I'm sure, is what drew the group which calls itself the Rainbow Family Tribal Council.

The Rainbow Family is an amorphous group once described by the Forest Service, the federal agency from time to time in contact or at least confrontation with the Rainbows, as "an informally organized, non-commercial organization with a national 'membership' of about 20,000." (Other descriptions by individual members of the Park Service will not be set forth herein since the portion of the Code of Judicial Conduct that permits us to write for publication makes it plain that we should not write anything which might detract from the dignity of the judiciary.) The Rainbows were first organized in 1970 in Oregon and have thereafter held an annual meeting variously described as a "reunion" or a "world peace gathering" or a "world peace and healing gathering" by those who attend. (Again, how it is described by some of the persons who do not attend but reside near the locations of such gatherings is beyond the scope of this text for the reasons set forth in the previous parenthetical.)

Now a few paragraphs ago when I described the gathering as taking place in July, if I had indulged in the ancient judicial tradition of peppering all writings with footnotes, I would have inserted a number and the diligent reader who followed that number to the bottom of the page would have read the following: "The first reported sighting of a Rainbow in the vicinity of the Nantahala National Forest actually occurred on or about May 26, 1987." As you might imagine, a gathering of several thousand hippies from across the country simply does not accidentally and spontaneously occur on the appointed day. So, while the 16th Annual Reunion occurred on schedule during the week of July 1-7, its harbingers preceded it as the robin oft in fact does the spring. As I have later gathered, the last act of each Rainbow reunion is a meeting of the council. The council consists of all those Rainbows who are still around the gathering place on that last day who decide that they are members of the council. They in council assemble. The last thing this council does is to decide the general vicinity of the next Rainbow reunion. Apparently the last act of the 15th Reunion in the Allegheny National Forest was a council determination that the 1987 event should be held in the deep southern

Appalachian Mountains somewhere around the convergence of Western North Carolina, East Tennessee, and North Georgia.

The Rainbows, it seems, always hold their reunions, whether in high hills or low dales, on land owned by the National Forest Service. Rumor has it that this is not so much because the Rainbows wish to avoid warfare with the owners of private property as it is because there are very few other land owners who have enough undeveloped land in one piece to accommodate the gathering. Also, the Rainbows may at least perceive that there is a dispute of criminal and civil jurisdiction between the federal and state governments over just who controls gatherings and offenses on Forest Service land. That dis-

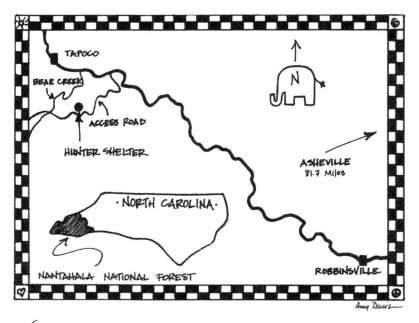

Amy Davis—

pute, I take it, is not because either government wishes to oust the other, but rather more closely parallels the history of a fictitious island created by Robert Benchley which he said was the subject of a war between Spain and Portugal. As I recall, Benchley reported that Spain lost and so had to take it.

Being all that as it may, the Rainbows had selected their general area, but the specific location depended upon the report of a small band that went ahead to search out the land. The word, I understand, is then spread by mailings to what I would describe as mail drops around the country and then by word of mouth to the Rainbow Family, its in-laws, outlaws, heirs, and assigns, to gather for a reunion in the woods commemorating and attempting to re-create the 1960s with all the love and loving, communing with nature, rejecting authority, accepting substances, and indulging appetites that made up the best and worst of that era.

In any event, since at their peak these gatherings sometimes include 20,000 or 30,000 people and since the sites are characterized by remoteness and many of those attending are characterized by a leftover '60s attitude toward regular employment and fixed abode, the seven days of the gathering and particularly the central date of July 4th represent not so much bounds as simply the peak in a temporary local population explosion that starts small, perhaps six weeks before the official gathering, and ends when some authority ousts the last remnant six weeks or so after its official end. I first learned of the impending explosion not by judicial notice, but through the newspapers, a way in which judges are not really supposed to learn much of anything even by those who suppose we learn much of anything in any fashion.

I first read of the gathering in early June. I then had no reason to believe that it involved me or to fear any taint of my pristine judicial mind by non-judicially received information. At that time, I was a United States District Court Judge in Asheville, North Carolina, the nearest permanently staffed federal court seat to the Nantahala National Forest. However, since no one had to my knowledge initiated any civil litigation concerning the gathering in my court and since criminal jurisdiction over the Forest is generally exercised by the State of North Carolina, I had no reason to suppose that it involved me or ever would. The biggest thing on my mind at the time was my own pending nomination to succeed Justice Antonin Scalia as a judge of the United States Court of Appeals for the District of Columbia Circuit. My nomination for that high court was held hostage by, among other senators, Kennedy of Massachusetts, Simon of Illinois, and Leahy of Vermont. I was going about my business as a U. S. District Judge while awaiting the will and pleasure of the great deliberative body on Capitol Hill.

In the meantime, my wife and I were getting ready to

attend the Fourth Circuit Judicial Conference. Statute required all active federal judges in five southeastern states to attend a three-day session commencing June 24. As I had my usual judicial business to pursue before that date, and since, contrary to popular belief, that business is rather time consuming, I only casually followed newspaper reports of a lawsuit brought in state court by Dr. Ronald H. Levine, the state health director for the State of North Carolina, to enjoin the holding of the reunion. While I thought the lawsuit was interesting and thought that someday I might look back into the relevant legal authorities, I had no reason to know that it would ever personally concern me so I put off a review of the questions involved for the leisure of a later day. I continued in that blissful state of ignorance until the day before my departure for the required conference. On that day, so the media had reported, the first hearing was scheduled to determine whether a North Carolina superior court judge would grant a restraining order temporarily halting a "mass gathering" of 5,000 or more people in the relevant location of the National Forest.

As my wife and I were retiring early that night in preparation for an early departure the next morning, the phone rang. When I answered it, the person on the other end requested me by name and mispronounced it. Now, most people who call you at home at night and mispronounce your name are pests. Most of these pests want to inform you that you've won a valuable prize, and you only need visit some new oceanside development to collect it. Some want you to buy tickets to a concern benefiting the fund to save something or other. But the most pesticide-resistant strain of such varmint is the reporter. That's what this varmint was. After I had admitted my identity, he asked when I would be holding a hearing. This caused two problems. In the first place, I cannot ethically discuss pending cases extra-judicially (extra-judicially doesn't mean involving extra judges, it means outside of court), and in the second place, I had no idea what case he was talking about. I did not think it would be terribly unethical to ask him that much.

"The Rainbow case," he said with a tone that at least implicitly suggested that I was far too great a simpleton to wear a black robe.

I further didn't think it terribly unethical to remind him that that case was in state court not mine.

"Oh," he retorted, "you haven't heard the news." I was afraid I was about to. "An ACLU lawyer is now representing the Rainbows. He's removed the case to federal court. Something about violating the constitutional rights to speech, assembly, and I don't know what all else."

I didn't know what all else either and simply told him I could not discuss the case. However, I could discuss the case with the lawyers for both sides. They called.

"When can you hear us?" they asked.

"I can't," I said. "All active federal judges are required to attend the Fourth Circuit Judicial Conference.

"However," I advised, "senior judges are not required to attend." (Senior judges are judges who have taken a qualified retirement. They remain available to hold court, often working very hard, but retain the freedom to work less than full time as their desires and infirmities may incline or compel them.)

"Judge Jones down in Rutherfordton is a senior judge and I don't believe he's planning on going this year." I politely ended the conversation and left the next day for the judicial conference in the blissful if ignorant belief that Judge Jones, a man of much wisdom and much understanding, would have solved all the problems attendant upon the 16th Annual Rainbow Family Reunion by the time of my return.

As you may have guessed, this is not exactly the way things developed.

2 ✦ THE BEGINNING OF WISDOM

On Monday, June 29, 1987, when I returned to my chambers (that's what we judges call our offices to distinguish us from lawyers), I found an Assistant Attorney General of the State of North Carolina and an attorney from the American Civil Liberties Union waiting for me. Each of them carried various court documents (officially called pleadings); each document was several pages thick; each had grown fat with the attachment of exhibits and illustrations; and each attorney announced that it was imperative that I immediately hold a hearing on whether or not the Rainbows could legally gather in the Nantahala National Forest. The State's attorney, a normally pleasant and unflustered ex-police officer named Bob, was loudly insisting that if I did not today grant a temporary restraining order, by July 4th possibly 20,000 "hippies" would be unlawfully assembled in the Nantahala National Forest. He insisted that they would be violating not only North Carolina's mass gathering law, but also every conceivable health and welfare regulation of the State of North Carolina, spreading disease, filth, contamination, and probably plague. Talking at approximately the same time, Mike, the civil liberties attorney, was insisting that if I did not deny the temporary restraining order, the State of North Carolina, acting in concert with the Forest Service of the United States, would be chilling, violating, dampening, and destroying his clients' constitutional rights to free speech, assembly, exercise of religion, and several others that I'm not sure are even in my copy of the Constitution.

At this point, though I find my chambers much more comfortable than a courtroom, I greatly wished for the order of a formal hearing. However, I did not convene one. Rather, I sat everyone down at my conference table, managed to get them talking one at a time (most of the time), and looked over the documents and attachments they piled before me. Unaccustomed as I am to saying nice things about the news media, most informative were various excerpts each side had clipped from local newspapers. It seems that Judge Jones had declined to hold the hearing, finding (I suppose reasonably) that I would be back in time to hear it, and that, therefore, there was no emergency calling for his services. The clippings further described what was going on in an area styled by the State's legal documents as "the vicinity of Forest Road development No. 62 (Slick Rock Road) and Bear Creek hunter shelter in the Cheoah District of the Nantahala Forest in Graham County, North Carolina." To help you visualize these goings-on, I now offer you a limited description of that vicinity (more details to follow later).

By way of introduction to that description, a Park Service document created after the 13th Annual Rainbow Reunion in California in July of 1984 compiled the common characteristics of the first fourteen gatherings. According to the Forest Service, common to all gatherings are:

1. Parking area – usually 1-2 miles from the actual site. People walk or shuttle to the site.

2. Bus Village – live-in vehicles park closer to the site for those that live out of their vehicles.

3. Kiddie Village – kitchen and day-care center for the kids, a festive and caring atmosphere.

4. MASH tent – medical center complete with doctor. They were really only capable of first-aid care. They treated a number of drug overdoses.

5. CALM (Center for Alterative Living Medicine) – holistic treatments with healers, masseuses and herbal medicine.

6. Communications Center – CB stations set up to monitor Forest Service and Law Enforcement activities as well as communicate among themselves. They also established a link with our Incident Command Center in case of need for Medivac.

These features were all present at the gathering in 1987. Specific to that gathering was the presence of but a single entrance to that section of the Nantahala National Forest where the main events were being held and the various campsites and kitchens and other features were located. That single access is by way of a winding dirt mountain road maintained by the Forest Service. It commences with a bridge across a small mountain river at the intersection of the Forest Service road-bridge and a public highway leading from Robbinsville to Tapoco. I gathered from the clippings and what I was advised by the attorneys in the case that the North Carolina Highway Patrol had set up a command post at that bridge and was attempting to exercise some degree of control of the ingress and egress. However, since this is public land and since the Rainbow gathering is hardly a recognized exclusive use and since no judge had issued a temporary restraining order, there wasn't much (if anything) the troopers could do to actually stop any person or persons from entering. I further noted, with some degree of interest, that at one point some Rainbows had chopped trees down across the road to prevent any more vehicles (including law enforcement vehicles) from entering. These had been removed.

I noted with a greater degree of interest that at some point during the coverage of the preliminary events, a naked woman had come running down the road and across the bridge pursued by four male Rainbows yelling for her to stop or she would get in trouble. She had not heeded these warnings but instead had taken the occasion to leap onto and jump up and down on the patrol car, and that she was finally arrested for possession of a felony amount of marijuana. (I was later advised by a reporter that he forwarded a photo of the leaping girl atop the blue light to the Commander of the Highway Patrol with the suggestion that he use it for the next year's recruiting poster. As far as I know, this suggestion was ignored.*) I had to ask. "How does a naked woman possess a felony quantity of marijuana?"

---

* That reporter, Bob Scott, graciously contributed a number of photographs for this book. Although Bob is now a captain in the sheriff's department of Macon County, North Carolina, I understand that he has yet to adopt his own suggestion.

"It seems it had something to do with the shirt she dropped as she was running out of the woods," one of the attorneys advised. "Hospital said she was on acid."

The papers further reported that among the myriad groups then gathering at Nantahala was a band of Hari Krishnas who it seems had brought their elephant. (More later on the elephant.)

I began to feel sufficiently up-to-date on the relevant facts and law to try to make some plans. "What is it exactly that you want the Court to do?" I asked the lawyers, pointing to them one at a time in the vain hope that we might achieve some order. "What am I supposed to hear at this hearing?"

"Judge, if you will look at our affidavits and pleadings," Bob said, "you'll see that North Carolina has a mass gatherings law."

I had looked and I had seen. Bob had attached a copy of the law to his complaint. That law, for any lawyers or law groupies who might be reading this, is §§ 130A-251 through 130A-258 of the North Carolina General Statutes. It recites the "intent and purpose" of the Legislature as being to "provide for the protection of the public health, safety and welfare of those persons in attendance at mass gatherings and of those persons who reside near or are located in proximity to the sites of mass gatherings or are directly affected by them."

In addition to not defining the difference between "residing near" and being "located in proximity to" the sites, the law doesn't tell us much about what it means in reference to those attending the mass gatherings who do not particularly want their health, safety, and welfare protected by the mass gatherings law.

It does, however, define a mass gathering as being a "congregation or assembly of more than 5,000 people in an open space or open air for a period of more than 24 hours." In addition to setting forth a lot of requirements to protect health, welfare, and so forth, such as regulating water supplies, toilet facilities, and emergency response centers, the law also requires an application at least 30 days in advance of any such planned event. It further requires the posting of a bond in the amount of $5,000 for the first "10,000 persons and an additional $1,000 for each additional 5,000 persons or fraction reasonably estimated to attend the mass gathering." (It doesn't say whether the fraction is of 5,000 or of a person, so I presumed it to be a fraction of 5,000.) It also requires the permittee to supply satisfactory evidence of liability and property damage insurance in an amount determined by a state official, up to $1,000,000. Finally (after a long, long list of detailed requirements ranging from parking to lighting to a few other pertinent ones I'll mention later), the law provides for methods of imposing upon the holder of the event and the holder's bond the costs of providing necessary facilities and law enforcement, repairing damages, and cleaning up after the event.

Needless to say, the Rainbows had applied for no such permit.

"If you'll look at our attached exhibits and affidavits," Bob continued, "you'll see that they have invited people from all over the United States and Canada. And, they're coming."

The attachments included several printed or neatly hand-lettered circulars apparently mailed out by the Rainbows or their advance party or their communications centers variously headed as

HOWDY FOLKS!

or

RAP I,

urging attendance at the gathering. Most of them bore the legend,

PLEASE DUPLICATE AND DISTRIBUTE FREELY.

One of them contained the Rainbow Family's own version of the necessary permit. That section of the "Rap" was as follows:

Permit To Gather Together

"CONGRESS SHALL MAKE NO LAW RESPECTING AN ESTABLISHMENT OF RELIGION OR PROHIBITING THE FREE EXERCISE THEREOF...
OR THE RIGHT OF THE PEOPLE TO PEACEABLY ASSEMBLE."
—From the 1st Amendment to the Constitution of the United States
"A freedom ain't a freedom unless we exercise it"

Bob continued, "Our evidence will show that based on past gatherings and present events, this reunion will inevitably exceed 5,000. We figure there were 2,500 or so by yesterday and they're coming in like lemmings."

"I think lemmings go out," interrupted one of my law clerks. (More on law clerks later. Much more.)

"Whatever," said Bob. "Hippies come in. And they're coming in droves."

Mike took his turn. "Our evidence will show that we're taking all necessary precautions to protect public health and welfare – doing everything the State asks in that connection; that we're a peaceful gathering. And that that law's unconstitutional anyway."

Bob retorted, "They're too close to the watershed of Tapoco, and they're going to pollute it."

"How," I asked, "am I going to hear enough evidence to decide anything before they've already exceeded 5,000 and maybe before the gathering's been held?"

The attorneys looked at each other and smiled. The smiles were a little sheepish. They disclosed to the experienced observer that the adverse parties had already discussed this question and that they had something in mind – something they were a little reluctant to tell the judge.

"Judge, did you ever hold a jury view?" Mike asked.

3 ✤ YOU'LL NEVER BELIEVE THE VIEW

A jury view for the uninitiated is a procedure where the trier of fact (in this case the judge, since this was a non-jury proceeding) takes evidence, not in the formal form of sworn testimony in a formal proceeding, but rather by traveling to the scene of whatever is in controversy and observing the evidentiary facts for itself (in this case himself). This procedure is usually used in cases where there is a dispute as to features of the land, such as easements, which are not readily established by testimony or exhibits which can practically be brought to the courtroom.

"I have," I said, "but I'm not sure one can be held in this case. I'm not interested in what either party can stage, or in attending a media event."

"We wouldn't want that either," the lawyers agreed. "But we would act in good faith and nobody would stage anything."

After some discussion on how to engineer a procedure for the viewing that would ensure its integrity, I exercised my prerogative as a federal judge and arbitrarily imposed my will. "If we're going, we're going right now," I ordered. "No one is to call ahead. No one is to use any means to alert his clients or the news media. We're going to see that place and those people as they are when we get there. Nobody is going to call me 'Judge.' Mike, you can pick two or three of your

Rainbow leaders and tell them who we are and they can show us around. But even they are to have no warning that we are coming. Bob, the same goes for your highway patrolmen." (The part about Mike's Rainbow "leaders" did cause a small conceptual difficulty since the Rainbows doctrinally eschew the concept of leaders, contending that all equally represent themselves and all equally lack authority to speak for the group.)

One of my law clerks then jumped into the conversation. By way of background, law clerks are attorneys employed to assist judges with matters of law, research, writing, and other essential high-level matters such as stuck zippers on robes and heavier files than the judge can carry to his car. While there are a few career law clerks in the federal judiciary, most are recent distinguished graduates of law schools who serve the judge for one or two years before going on to distinguished careers in practice where within two or three years they make more money than the judge does. It is often said that the judge carries much of his legal knowledge in the heads of his law clerks. I was at that time carrying much of my legal knowledge in the heads of two young recent law school graduates, Beth and Melanie. Melanie immediately objected to a detail of my plan.

"Judge," she said, "we can't go right now, Beth and I can't walk around in those woods in high heels and skirts."

Before I could respond, Mike did.

"That won't be any problem at the Rainbow gathering. When we get to the place where we have to park, a lot of the people will be barefoot and naked anyway; you can just join them."

I thought he was kidding. I could tell from Beth's expression that she wasn't so sure.

I had a different response to the problem. "I really hadn't thought of you going."

Melanie took issue. "Judge, you know that circumstances in a place like that could cause you and one of the lawyers to be separated from the other lawyer. That shouldn't occur without a witness to establish your neutrality. To be sure, you'd have to have both of us. Besides that, if you have to write an opinion on this in a hurry, you're going to need our help."

Melanie was right, and I consented to their going along. I modified my order to say that Bob, Mike, and I would leave right then. I also commandeered an Assistant United States Attorney and directed him that because of the federal ownership of the National Forest he would be appearing as *amicus curiae* and would go with us to protect the government's interests. An *amicus curiae* is a friend of the court and he didn't look very friendly right then, but he did go along. He and I and the two other attorneys were to travel in Bob's car since it was equipped with a Highway Patrol radio and he could assure us access to parking and to the Forest Service road. The law clerks would follow a little later in Melanie's car after they had gone home and changed shoes and clothes.

During the two-hour drive to Nantahala Forest, I learned more about the lawsuit and discussed more about the logistics of the jury view with the lawyers. I knew from those conversations and the newspapers' reports that the common practice now was for troopers to control vehicular access to the Forest Service road. Cars of arriving Rainbows were parked along the state highway in the general vicinity of its intersection with the bridge. (It's a "T" intersection with the Forest Service road-bridge forming the shank and the state highway the crossbar.) Live-in vehicles were being permitted to enter and a permit system had been worked out for some other vehicles to come and go. Things apparently were incredibly peaceful. The troopers were arresting those who committed violations around the bridge, or in sight of the highway, such as smoking pot or skinny-dipping in the river, but things were much more lax in the encampment, the near border of which was a couple of miles up the Forest Service road.

The Rainbows, I learned, were objecting to even the presence of the law enforcement officers at the gate across the bridge, insisting that they could control access. They were also operating a shuttle from a shady lean-to just on the forest side of the bridge up to the main encampment. I envisioned the shuttles as being old school buses, but later learned they consisted of two makeshift pickup trucks more reminiscent of the *Grapes of Wrath* than of anything Ford or GMC may have made lately.

When we were about ten minutes from the bridge, Bob radioed ahead to the troopers that we needed two parking spaces at the bridge.

"We'll reserve 'em," the radio crackled back. "What happened in court?"

Bob was careful not to reveal anything I didn't want him to. "I'll tell you when I get there," he said.

Before we got there – indeed a couple of miles before we got there – we began to see cars parked on both sides of the road. While I can't say we saw license plates from every state in the Union (I never saw Hawaii) or every province of Canada, I can say that we certainly saw a random sampling. From the farthest out of those cars, people were pouring out. All were moving in the same direction, toward the bridge. When we got to the bridge, we saw a similar flow of people coming down the highway from the other direction. We saw hitch-hikers dismounting at the bridge. We saw one or two live-in vehicles being given access across the bridge. Bob had been right. But for the direction of the flow, it looked like lemmings.

Well, really, it didn't look like lemmings. It looked like people acting like lemmings, except that I've never imagined lemmings as being that happy. What it really looked like was the late 1960s all in one place and moving toward one goal. There were people in blue jeans and T-shirts. Some blue jeans were cutoffs. Some T-shirts were tie-dyed; some were decorated with flowers; and some bore political slogans. The only difference between the summer of 1987 and the '60s (or early '70s) was the nature of the slogans. Instead of calling for making love and not war, they now sought to "IMPEACH MEESE, BUSH, REAGAN." (I don't think it ever dawned on Mike or any of his clients that I had been appointed to my district judgeship by Reagan and nominated to the D.C. Circuit by the same President. I don't really believe it would have mattered to him or me if it had.)

There were people in beads and leather and quasi-Indian garb. (I later saw a fellow at the campsite who was actually wearing a fur helmet with buffalo horns.) There were women in long cotton dresses; girls and men in worn-smooth buckskin. There were people with flowers in their hair.

But more on all those later when we get to the camp. At this point we were getting to the bridge. There were several troopers in apparent control of the bridge and there were parking spaces occupied by law enforcement cars. Some spaces were saved with signs saying "Reserved for Official Vehicles," one of which Bob chose. As we got out of the car, I told the lawyers again, "No one is to call me 'Judge.'" One of the troopers turned around.

"Judge," he said, "what are you doing here?"

The trooper was a neighbor of mine in Asheville. Since his name is Bob, he will henceforth be known as "my neighbor" to avoid confusion. That bridge was a good two hour's drive beyond the normal bounds of his assigned territory. I could have asked him the same question. However, I realized its answer just by looking around. My neighbor and all the other troopers at the bridge were men past 40 with gray in their hair and a lot of years on the road. I suspected then and confirmed later that most of them were veterans of an event in the early '70s called the "Love Valley Love-In" – a not-so-mini Woodstock held in North Carolina. None of these men needed to get their blackjacks out to prove they were men. None of these troopers needed to make an arrest just to prove they were troopers. I realized then how North Carolina had kept things as peaceful as they had at the bridge and I renewed my respect for Bob, the Assistant Attorney General, whom I learned had suggested the personnel assignments for this particular event.

We shushed my neighbor, asked him to call me "Dave," and explained what we were doing. Now, we knew that I was not about to pass as a member of the Rainbows. Although I had taken off my jacket and tie, the clean dress slacks, well-polished boots, and a hat eccentrically Western by design but unmistakeably new and fairly expensive in character, just served as badges of the outsider. But we did have hopes that my "secret identity" would not be too rapidly spread through the camp.

My neighbor brought us up to date. "We figure," he said, "that there were at least 3,000 of them in there by noon today." (It was then about half past noon.)

"You know the Hari Krishnas are here?" he asked.

"I understand they brought their elephant," one of us commented.

"Yeah," my neighbor said. "You know how hard it is to find somebody to keep your elephant when you're out of town."

"How did they get that damned elephant in there?" I

asked.

"Well, they had a real problem," my neighbor explained. "It was a pretty big rig they had her loaded on and it couldn't have gone around those curves among the pine trees. The Krishna that was driving the rig couldn't even get it turned around in the road and backed onto the bridge. So I backed it across the bridge for 'em and they unloaded the elephant and walked her up the road."

There is nothing like troopers with gray in their hair to know how to keep the peace.

We waited a few minutes for the law clerks to arrive. They didn't. We decided it was time to go up the winding road to the encampment. 🐘

Part II

In the Camp
of the Rainbows

4 ⚬ WELCOME HOME

Bob radioed up to the camp to some law officer stationed there that we were coming and to hold the shuttle since two vehicles cannot meet on the little Forest Service road. The troopers waved the foot travelers on the bridge to one side and we drove in. As we crossed the bridge and just before we passed through a Forest Service gate, we saw to the left of the road a big homemade sign reading, **WELCOME HOME !** To the right stood a make-shift structure of wooden poles and canvas labeled "SHUTTLE STOP 1." Some of the people crossing the bridge were gathering around the shelter, but most, although it was a very hot day, were electing to hike the two miles or so up the steep mountain road. As we drove on, we passed a constant stream of them.

According to a hand-drawn map that Mike had apparently obtained from his clients, our first goal was an area labeled "WELCOME CENTER" at a second Forest Service gate, normally setting off a recreation area a few square miles in dimension but now claimed as the temporary home of the Rainbows. The map showed the location of various "camps," "kitchens," and "meadows," apparently given names by their occupants according to their uses. Outside the bounds defined by the gate at the Welcome Center, only two specific sites were marked, Shuttle Stop 1 and a dot designated "SHUTTLE STOP 2 (ALCOHOL CAMP)." I did not feel that I then

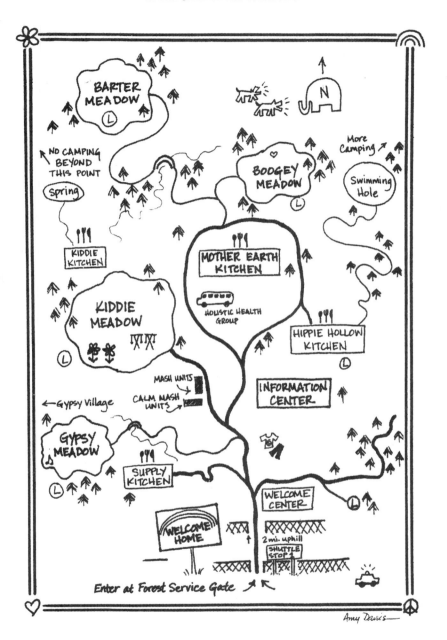

dared ask the reason for the designation "ALCOHOL CAMP" on a Forest Service site in a dry county. I later learned that it is a goal of the Rainbows that alcohol use be strongly discouraged, and those who found it absolutely necessary were requested to confine it to that area outside the main encampment. As we passed that camp, we saw no alcohol, however.

What we did see there and all the way up the mountain was a continuing stream of the same sort of eclectically dressed and decorated people we had seen at the road. Many were wearing backpacks or carrying blanket rolls. Several had given up at Shuttle Stop 2 and were sitting back in the shady forest awaiting transportation. As I said, it was a very hot day, and we saw one young man in cut-off blue jeans carrying a plastic bag of ice. I'm sure the ice did not make it to the encampment, but I'm also sure he was a lot more comfortable going up the road for having spent whatever he spent at some convenience store back on the highway.

When we finally reached the area called "Welcome Center," we were welcomed. Very welcomed. In addition to the Forest Ranger

> **DRUGS:**
> AS A FAMILY WE DIS-
> COURAGE DRUGS AND
> ENCOURAGE SACRAMENTS,
> UNDERSTANDING THAT
> THERE ARE MANY
> DIFFERENCES BETWEEN THE
> TWO. MANY IN THE FAMILY
> DO NOT CONSIDER ALCOHOL
> AND MAN MADE CHEMICALS
> TO BE SACRAMENTS. GENTLE
> HEALING HERBS ARE. INTOX-
> ICATION CAN BE DANGEROUS
> TO THE SPIRIT OF OUR
> GATHERING.

who had taken Bob's radio communication and pulled the rag-tag shuttles to the side of the road, an apparently official (as official as anything could be at a Rainbow gathering) welcoming party of a half-dozen people stood at the gate dispensing hand-drawn maps, oral directions, and a semi-constant chorus of "Welcome Home." A plump woman hugged Mike, called him by name, and proudly displayed to him a new T-shirt neatly stenciled, **WELCOME HOME !**

"You ought to get you one of these shirts over at the Barter Meadow," she told him.

He allowed that he might and then asked for a couple of people by name. Now I should note at this point that some of the Rainbows had nice, normal, everyday names like Bonnie Sue Phillips, David Moore, and Garrick Beck. Others go by such names as Stephen Principle, Thomas Conscientious Objector, or May Love & Peace. Still others give only first names and others are known by such names as Badger, Honey Bear, and Moon Unit. The woman who welcomed us was, I believe, Joanee Freedom, but I always think of her as Welcome Woman.

Anyway, Mike and the welcoming committee were able to round up a couple of the apparent leaders (whether or not accepting the title). I believe it was Garrick Beck and Stephen Principle, though I'm satisfied that names did not matter very much. They and I and the lawyers, together with the woman who had led the welcome, found as much privacy as we could behind one of the shuttle vehicles and discussed what to do next. We thought it was necessary to let these guides know who I was and what I was about so that they could lead me to the areas most appropriate to observe the health and welfare precautions proudly undertaken by the Rainbows and the health and welfare dangers solemnly omened by the State.

I asked the guides, "Since none of us are dressed a lot like," I searched for a word, not knowing if "hippies" would be offensive, and finally continued, "Rainbows, will everybody know what's up?"

"No," Garrick assured me. "We have publicly offered local people – even officials – guided tours of the gathering. Quite a few have actually come. You won't attract any attention."

I didn't believe that last part, but I decided to proceed with the "jury view" for whatever degree of accuracy it might actually have.

I was concerned at that point that if we began the tour, my law clerks might never see us again. But if we delayed the tour, that was more time for the word about who we were and what was going on to spread throughout the camp. All three attorneys agreed that it was not appropriate for me to be conducted alone with any one of them, but all three consented to my being conducted about the camp alone while they went back down to the bridge to meet my law clerks, bring them back up and catch us later. The attorneys went – I think happily – back towards civilization. I went on – not without trepidation – in the company of Welcome Woman, Garrick, and Principle in search of the relevant facts about the 16th Annual Rainbow Reunion.

"What are you most interested in seeing?" one of them asked me.

"I had been afraid you would ask me that." But I had to come up with an answer. Mentally, I cataloged the points of contention. The State was concerned about drinking water, disposal of human wastes, sanitation in food processing, the medical needs of the campers, and the welfare of children.

"First, I guess, anything related to water use and, uh, waste disposal," I told them.

Garrick thought a second. "Human waste disposal or trash and garbage?"

I had not thought of trash and garbage. "Both, I guess."

"Okay," one of them said. "Let's go."

They showed me their water system, which ran throughout the camp. They had brought in black plastic pipe and run it from the mountain streams and high springs by gravity feed to cocks at each of the kitchens, major campsites, and a few other designated locations. Beside each of the taps, in compliance with their own practice from prior gatherings and a request from the State of North Carolina, they had posted signs reading,

"CAUTION: SURFACE WATER [or in appropriate cases, SPRING WATER], BOIL BEFORE USING."

"We really don't think," Garrick said, "that boiling is necessary in the case of the spring water. But the State insists that it is and we see no reason not to post the signs. We think the spring water is pure enough, but we're happy to go along." He smiled.

In fact the signs were very important even as to the spring water. That particular section of mountains is, as it happens, inhabited by wild hogs, locally called Russian boars. Those hogs are not native to the mountains but were imported during the 19th century by wealthy sportsmen who released them in the mountain lands to hunt, without knowledge of or concern for the damage that they have since done to the ecology. Their habit is to make wallows of any open spring they find. As it happens, these swine are commonly host to shigellæ, a genus of nonmotile aerobic bacteria that, when ingested by humans, causes shigellosis, a particularly virulent form of dysentery. The Rainbows believed that boiling spring water was unnecessary since they had piped their spring water not from open springs, but from new springs they dug out and lined. What they apparently did not reckon is that the springs they had dug out are water tables which become open springs in wetter weather (hence the mountain expression "wet weather springs"). Therefore, the hogs have wallowed in the same water supply during wetter times. The shigellæ are present down into the ground. Some of them are still alive, albeit in infinitesimal numbers. Even an infinitesimal number of shigellæ — I'm told the number that can survive in a quantity of feces attaching to a single foot of a fly — is sufficient to spread shigellosis.

Many of the Rainbow campers, in the belief boiling spring water was unnecessary, didn't boil it, but drank the cool, refreshing liquid directly from the black plastic pipes. Shortly after the end of the gathering, shigellosis appeared, I understand, in all fifty states, traceable to the Rainbow gathering. Now it's probably true that every case of shigellosis in the country was attributed to that source whether or not such attribution was in fact correct. Nonetheless, I suppose Dr. Levine and the rest of the North Carolina health officials feel very vindicated. But that's getting ahead of the story, and probably does not belong in this story at all.

After examining the water supply, I told them I wanted to see some of their latrines. Actually, I did not want to see any of their latrines, but I felt I should. We walked across a small ridge since the campers, both by Rainbow custom and in keeping with the requests of the State, separated their latrines from water sources and carefully did not construct them uphill from any water sources. The latrine was a slit trench. One of my guides showed me a Marine Corps publication describing how to build field latrines and informed me that they had fully complied with the Marine Corps instructions.

This may have been true insofar as the length, width and depth of the trench, but I noted one important particular in which Rainbows and Marines differ. The Marine literature recommends screening the latrine with canvas. Rainbows do not screen their latrines with anything. Since I later learned that many of the people in the Rainbow gathering have regular jobs they work at all year long and take only a week or two vacation to go back and be hippies in the summer, there is something there I don't understand.

If I had only a week or two of vacation a year, I really would have little desire to spend it in a place where my only toilet facilities were unscreened latrines. I would have even less desire to spend it with several thousand other people whose only toilet facilities were unscreened latrines. There are certain necessary functions which are not like justice. We say in the law that justice should not only be done, it should be seen to be done. Certain functions which must be done should not be seen to be done. Personally, I always averted my eyes when our kitten was using the sandbox. But as my Grandma always said, "To each his own."

By the latrine hung a sign reading "COVER WITH ASHES. COVER ASHES WITH DIRT." A large barrel full of ashes stood by the sign.

Also displayed was a smaller paper which was a copy of the Rainbows' Rap 107. The relevant portion of the "Rap" was outlined in red:

PROTECT OUR HEALTH!
USE YOUR OWN BOWL AND SPOON.
USE ONLY S__ITERS AND COVER
S__T AND PAPER WITH DIRT AND
ASHES; WASH HANDS.(BREAK THE
FLY CONNECTION:S__T-FLY-FOOD-YOU!)

(The blanks are mine, Rainbows are less decorous than judges.)

"We gather the ashes from the fires every evening and accumulate them at the latrines," Welcome Woman told me.

"Good idea," I said, and hastily started away from the latrine before anyone came to use it.

5 ⚜ OF BUMPERS & BABIES, KITCHENS & CAMPS

We went on a few hundred more yards and they showed me more parts of their water system and another latrine (again, thankfully, not in use). We came back to the continuation of the Forest Service road which extended on into the camping area, another three or four miles past the entry gate, forking in places, forks ending in others. I saw live-in vehicles from classically decorated hippie vans to old school buses parked all down one side of the road, and on both sides of the wider places. Like the cars along the highway, they bore license plates from what seemed to be any and every state. Also like the cars, only more so, they exhibited bumper stickers and painted slogans of near-infinite variety. I came out of a political background. I have been to a lot of political rallies. Of course, as a federal judge, all that is in my past. Politically we are a bit like eunuchs. We are unable to participate in the fun because we are dedicated to protecting it for everyone else. But given my past history, I'm no stranger to bumper stickers. Around the conservative political gatherings that were once my principal habitat, I thought I had seen a wide variety of stickers. After coming to the Rainbow camp, I knew I was wrong. These messages ranged from the ridiculous, "SAVE THE HOUSE FLY," to the sublime, "OBEY GOD." From the obscure, "BILBO BAGGINS LIVES," to the obscene " ... " (I told you I could not write anything that would detract from the dignity of the judiciary) – with everything in between. I was mildly surprised to find several that would have been at home at my old conservative gatherings, including a large number describing abortion as "THE ULTIMATE CHILD ABUSE."

We had started at my request toward a location on the map labeled "MOTHER EARTH KITCHEN," which was the nearest to the Welcome Center of any of the main features of the gathering. We were then still very near the point where we had come in. We spotted among the live-in vehicles one with an awning outside extending away from the road next to a little meadow. This vehicle was a large, nice, if obviously used, motor home having front and rear doors. Over the front door hung a sign, "HOLISTIC HEALTH GROUP." Over the rear, "LABOR UNIT."

"Hey," one of my guides said, "you're interested in our health and welfare. We'll take you to the CALM – MASH unit later, but this is an interesting little outfit."

Welcome Woman pulled me over to the RV and introduced me to a couple under the awning who were playing with a naked toddler. I noted that the introduction complied perfectly with my instructions that I was to be called only "Dave," and not "Judge."

"This is Dave," she said. "He's having a tour of the camp."

The woman under the awning excitedly showed me inside where there was, I must say, an impressive midwifery unit. She told me, "We usually have one or two babies delivered at each gathering." She patted her daughter on the head and said, "I had hoped she'd be born at the last one, but she was a little early."

"She and I are both midwives," the man with her told me. While I had no reason to doubt him, I would have supposed him to be a midhusband, but I guess there is no such thing.

After they handed me a sheet telling me what to do if I began labor in the camp, we continued toward Mother Earth Kitchen. This entailed passing through a little meadow where a sign read "FUTURE HOME OF MOONDANCERS." In the center of the meadow, a half-dozen male Rainbows were building what appeared to be a stage of poles and boards. One of them was wearing nothing but a pair of J.C. Penney work boots while he was swinging a hammer – sledgehammer, that is – to drive pegs into the ground. I thought of Beth and Melanie and wondered how long it would be before the other non-Rainbows caught up with me.

The way to Mother Earth Kitchen led down a path in the woods which, by its well-worn appearance, predated the arrival of the Rainbows. However, the constant stream of people up and down the path was obviously wearing it worse. I thought at that point of an objection to the gathering that Kip, the Assistant U.S. Attorney, had raised.

I should note, I suppose, that despite Kip's reluctance to enter the case, he was quite up-to-date on the subject of the gathering and, in fact, had been in near-constant contact with the Forest Service since the sighting of the first Rainbow. He – Kip that is, not the Rainbow – had pointed out that the more the paths were worn the more erosion would occur when the then-current drought finally broke. I raised this with the Rainbows, who assured me that they would periodically heap leaves on all paths and would fully cover them in the weeks following the official gathering. They pointed out to me places where they had lain fallen trees or limbs across the path to further retard the erosion.

Sporadically, campers met or passed us and we met

or passed them. Many of them stopped to hug one or more of our little group.

It was, as I had mentioned, a very hot day and many of the men had taken off their shirts. Many of the women had, too. Now when I say many of the women had taken off their shirts, I do not mean that they were showing their bras. In fact, during my entire contact with the Rainbow reunion, I do not recall seeing any woman with or without a shirt who appeared to be wearing a bra. One of the many evidences of sexual equality at a Rainbow reunion is that men do not wear bras and women don't either. As it happens, the Rainbow reunion was the first time I had ever been in a society in which large numbers of women exercised the option of going topless. I had always supposed, naively as it develops, that toplessness, like fashions in a more conventional society, would generally be adopted by those women who looked most attractive in that particular fashion. This is not the case. I saw no correlation at all. Indeed, I don't know why I ever supposed it. Men have never shown much connection between going without shirts and looking good that way. It doesn't take a trip to a hippie festival to find that out. A drive through suburbia at lawn-mowing time is quite sufficient. At the Rainbow reunion, I found out the same is true of women. (As time went on, I learned that the same applies to total nudity, both male and female.)

However, the members of our little group kept our

shirts on and continued down the path toward Mother Earth Kitchen. On either side of the path were little individual campsites with tents, lean-tos and sometimes just exposed bedding rolls, wherever someone had found room enough to put one down. At last we came to Mother Earth Kitchen to conduct my inspection.

Mother Earth Kitchen lay to the right of the path down a fairly steep bank. The proprietors had used limbs and poles to make a rough staircase to what looked like the Hollywood concept of a hobo kitchen. A tarpaulin supported by eight poles shaded an area framed by a square of rough planks about counter high. A small stack of what looked like schoolhouse plates stood next to a sign reading, "PLEASE BRING YOUR OWN – WE DON'T HAVE MANY DISHES." Three buckets of liquid stood in what was apparently the dishwashing area, two labeled "BLEACH – DISINFECT" and one, "CLEAN WATER RINSE." Five or six people within the enclosure were busily stacking things, mixing things, and generally getting ready for an anticipated rush of customers. One of the black pipes ran to a stop-cock over a large water tub with the usual instructions about boiling. One of my guides introduced me to a large, smiling, dimpled woman who appeared to be in charge.

"Dave, this is Mother. Mother, this is Dave. He lives here in Western North Carolina and we're giving him the tour."

"Welcome home," said Mother.

Mother was one of the women who proved my earlier observations about the universal availability of the toplessness option. Other than a pair of high-topped tennis shoes, she was wearing nothing but cut-off jeans with a broad leather Western belt. She did not have the figure I would once have expected to go with that style. Without writing anything indelicate, I will just say that Mother's figure made it impossible to read the buckle on her Western belt.

While I was trying to think of something appropriate to say, she stepped from behind the make-shift counter and hugged me. "Welcome home," she said again.

"Uh, I'd like to see your, uh, kitchen," I stammered.

"Here it is!" she said, gesturing openhandedly.

"Show him your oven," said Welcome Woman.

Mother led me to a clean oil drum propped up on its side atop rocks leaving room for a significant bed of coals underneath. Hard-baked mountain clay mostly covered the outside of the drum. "Was it ever used for oil?" I asked.

They all chuckled. "No," said Mother. "We rig up a lot of kinds of ovens for these wonderful gatherings, but at the common kitchens, we're all careful about sanitation and human safety."

Garrick expanded on her comments. "We ask everyone to bring their food to the common kitchens where we have the good wash setups and where we know the preparation will be safe. Of course, not all of them do, but most people want to. That way you can eat in good company and enjoy it a lot more while being assured that everything is safe."

Concededly, Garrick knew who I was and why I was there. I'm convinced Mother did not.

They showed me a big eating area where logs and rocks had been arranged for maximum comfortable seating, another wash area not yet in use but ready for the larger crowd later. Mother offered me some fresh baked bread and water which they swore had been boiled. (Well, they really didn't swear, but they did assure me it had been boiled. I couldn't have administered an oath without revealing my secret identity.) The day was hot and dusty. I had not eaten since a light breakfast. A judge must avoid all risk of prejudice. This includes avoiding the appearance of prejudice. If I ate the bread or drank the water and thereafter came down with diarrhea, I might appear to be prejudiced. I might also appear to be uncomfortable. If I came down with diarrhea before leaving the Rainbow camp and had to repair to their latrines, I might appear to be embarrassed. If I ate the bread and drank the water and nothing happened, I might appear to be prejudiced the other way. I refused as politely as I could without letting Mother know why. We went back to the trail through an easier access at the lower side of the eating area. It was on a near level with the trail so that cut out steps were not necessary. "Where do we go next?" Welcome

Woman asked.

Garrick, Principle and I studied the map. "About a half mile on down," Garrick suggested, "there's another kitchen. It's called 'Hippie Hollow' and you might take a look at it. Just below that and off to the side there is another latrine or two."

We headed down toward Hippie Hollow. The further down the trail we got the more people we met and passed coming and going up and down the hill. After we had gone around two or three more turns through the thickly wooded park, we began to meet a few Rainbows who had taken off more than their shirts. These people were naked. I do not mean they were naked to the waist. Well, of course, they were naked to the waist, but they were naked from the waist also. These people were naked. The further down we went the more naked people there were. Many of them were wet. All of us were wet with sweat. But these people were wet!

We came to Hippie Hollow. Like Mother Earth, it had a hobo kitchen, sitting area, and a tap on the black pipeline. We inspected it, and then went to a latrine over a small ridge.

On our way, I had been glancing at the little campsites along the path and around the kitchens. Most people had left little of value at the sites, perhaps partly in response to advice in one of the "Raps" to

WATCH YOUR GEAR ~ "TEMPT NOT LEST YE BE LIFTED FROM."

But one thing of practical value I noticed in more than one campsite – a roll of toilet paper. At the latrine behind Hippie Hollow, we had the experience I'd been dreading. That latrine was in use. A young woman wearing only a blue work shirt was squatting at one end of the latrine. Her back was to us and the work shirt was pulled up around her waist. She held a roll of paper in one hand. "Hi, Honey," said one of my guides. "This is Dave, he's having a tour."

"Welcome home," she said in a strained voice, and finished her business. Well, I assume she finished it. I got away from there as quickly as I could.

6 ✤ *OF HIPPIES, HOLLOWS & HOLES*

As we came back past the kitchen toward the trail, I looked back at the Hippie Hollow sign. "That name, Hippie Hollow, reminds me of a place in Texas back in the '60s," I said. "But it wasn't a campsite or kitchen, it was just sort of a swimming hole on the back of a lake near Austin."

"I remember it," said Welcome Woman. "And did you go swimming at Hippie Hollow?" she asked me.

At this point, three things went through my mind. First, people at Hippie Hollow, whether or not I ever went there, rarely wore bathing suits. Second, I know my rights and I did not have to answer her question. Third, I was not under oath and if I did answer her question, I would not get into any trouble if I didn't tell the truth.

At this point you may well ask yourself two questions. First, what answer did he give to her question? Second, was that answer true? In response to your questions, I would say first, I still know my rights and I do not have to answer your questions either. If I did answer it, I'm not under oath and I wouldn't get in any trouble if I did not tell the truth.

This line of discussion stirred a comment from Principle. "Our swimming hole is another three-quarters of a mile down this path."

"It doesn't show on the map," I said.

Principle took the map. He took my pen out of my shirt pocket and drew a circle at the bottom of the map which he labeled "SWIMMING HOLE."

"Now it shows on the map," said Principle. "If you are looking at water use, you probably ought to inspect it too."

I didn't disagree. I didn't agree either. But we walked on down the trail. The trail was still steep, still winding, still hot, and still dusty. We were still hot and still dusty. We met more and more hippies. More and more of them were wet. More and more of them were naked. They looked a good deal more comfortable than I felt.

As we neared what appeared to be the end of the trail, I saw no swimming hole. I saw only a stand of hardwoods. I could hear running water some short distance away, along with the tingling shouts and laughter that you always hear around any swimming hole. I had seen a mountain stream running roughly parallel to the trail in that same direction all the way down the trail. It had curved sharply away from us a few hundred yards back. "This way," said Principle, and led me that way.

We went via a tiny side trail into the stand of trees just as two wet young women wearing tennis shoes, backpacks and broad smiles stepped through from the other side. Otherwise naked people look strange wearing tennis shoes and backpacks. They did not look bad, only strange. After you think about it, they looked sensible. The tennis shoes help about sharp rocks, thorns and other obstacles on the path. The backpack helps about being lifted from. That is, what you can't leave in your camp without tempting lifters, you can't carry in your pockets if you don't have pockets. But that realization comes only when you think about it. When I saw the two smiling wood nymphs in their backpacks and tennis shoes, I wasn't thinking about sensible considerations. They looked strange, but they did not look bad. After they passed and as I looked back over my shoulder at the backpackers, my guides pulled me along the side trail and through the stand of trees into a broad mountain meadow. On the far side of the meadow was another stand of trees. I could hear the water and the laughter a little more clearly.

I learned at that point that the Rainbows use their

swimming holes much the way apartment dwellers use their swimming pools. That is, they don't really do much swimming. What they do is get in the water to get wet and cool off. Then they get out and lay down in the sun. Apartment dwellers generally do this on some sort of decking around the pool. Rainbows were doing it in the meadow. The other difference was that apartment dwellers wear bathing suits when they cool off and sun. Rainbows don't. While I admit that I did not count, there must have been two dozen naked couples sprawled on the grass in various degrees of wet, along with another dozen or so detached individuals. One lovely black girl who appeared to be about six months pregnant was sitting semi-lotus fashion in the middle of the meadow, her head laid back while a young man, naked as herself, rubbed her back with a flower. I did not ask why he rubbed her back with a flower, and I have never found out.

Four men were standing up going through some sort of exercise under the direction of a bearded older man of East Indian appearance.

But I had not come to inspect their bodies, but rather their water use. We walked through the next stand of trees to the swimming hole.

The swimming hole was of course a portion of the little mountain stream. The Rainbows had done what I have often seen young Indians do on the nearby Cherokee Reservation. They had found a place where there was a natural hole in the creek bed, that is, where the water slowed at the foot of an incline so that it widened and deepened for quieter, more pleasant, use. Then they had taken rocks from the bottom of the hole and built a partial dam on the downstream side. Therefore, each time you move a rock, you have a double effect on deepening the swimming hole and increasing its size. The Indians have done it for years, and, in fact, we used to do it in the countryside outside Asheville when I was growing up. It has no long-range detrimental effect on the ecology whatsoever, and it did not disturb me that the Rainbows had done what we natives, American Indian and white alike, have been doing for generations. Several campers were playing in the water. Some would leave the water and go back and lie down. But at any given time, there were a dozen or so naked, happy hippies in the water. It was a hot, dry day. Welcome Woman looked up at me. "Dave," she said, "you look awfully hot. Why don't you take a swim."

I knew if I did, the next day's papers were likely to bear headlines something to the effect of "SENTELLE JOINS RAINBOWS – SAYS 'TO HELL WITH THE D.C. CIRCUIT.'"

Also, I kept thinking about Beth and Melanie coming along back there somewhere. "No," I said. "I don't think so, but you feel free." She didn't. A few of the swimmers did splash water on her.

We walked back through the meadow. As we did,

I noticed how white some of the buns had been that were turned up toward the sun and how red they were becoming. This being a Rainbow could be a most uncomfortable way of life.

We struggled back up the steep path. Just below Hippie Hollow, we came around the bend and met Mike, Bob, Kip, and my law clerks. They all looked hot. Beth looked sort of dazed. Melanie looked happy. Bob looked like he was about to burst out laughing.

They turned back uphill and we all started back toward the main encampment to continue our tour.

Bob pulled me aside. Now I recognize when the attorney for one side in a lawsuit pulls the judge aside, sometimes he is seeking to curry some sort of improper favor. I knew instinctively that this was not such a time. Lawyers attempting to curry favor do not have tears standing in their eyes as they shake from suppressed laughter. "Judge," he exploded in my ear, "it was worth the trip out here to see Beth's face when the first naked guy came walking out of the woods. You could have stood on one of her eyeballs and cut the other one off with a chainsaw."

7 ⚶ ON "CALM – MASH" & NOT-SO-CALM OBSERVERS

I suppose in good sportsmanship I should have invited the rest of our party back down the hill to the swimming hole. But I'd already seen that and there was a lot more camp to inspect.

When we finally got back to the top of the trail at the Forest Service road which ran along the ridge, I looked again at the long line of live-in vehicles. One in particular drew my attention.

Three couples were busily setting up an awning, which many of the live-ins had, and unpacking boxes. They had obviously just arrived. Already, though, they had unpacked some loud speakers, and I do mean loud. Their electric music was jarringly inappropriate in the Nantahala Forest, Rainbow gathering or no Rainbow gathering.

I've been in trial law most of my adult life. In some ways that's a lot like playing poker. You learn not to let your expression reveal your feelings. This time I think I failed.

"They just got here," said Garrick. "By nightfall, their neighbors will have gently convinced them that electric amplifiers aren't welcome here. Music's welcome," he continued, "but usually only acoustic."

By the time we came back through there a few hours later, the amps had been packed up and the audio show was over.

The Rainbows are a lot like city planners in one way. They had already put up throughout the encampment a lot of signs with arrows. We saw some that directed us to such locations as "BOOGEY MEADOW," about which

I've always wondered but never asked, "LATRINES," and "SWIMMING HOLE." Several, however, pointed in one direction, away from the sites I'd already seen. These included "CALM – MASH UNITS," "KIDDIE MEADOW," and "BARTER MEADOW." Since the first two of these were on my "must see" list, we headed in that direction. We climbed a short, steep hill, and went about a quarter-mile through the woods on an up-and-down path with roughly the configuration of a small roller coaster. Finally, we came to a place where the forest parted onto the largest meadow I'd seen all day. On the lower, near side of the meadow, was a small pole-and-canvas-awning structure labeled "INFORMATION CENTER." My guides led me to that center first.

I don't remember the names of the man and woman they introduced me to there. Since the man replaced Garrick as one of my guides from there on, I'll give him the name "Ralph" for convenience, but I don't think it's the name they gave me. Whatever his name, he and a lovely young woman were giving out information. They greeted newcomers with a hearty "Welcome Home," provided directions, and when appropriate distributed handouts labeled "Rap" giving details of not exactly "rules" but rather expected behavior concerning the care of children (of which there were many in the camp), dogs (of which there were more), and locations of kitchens, the CALM – MASH units, and so forth. Posted at the Information Center were copies of North

Carolina's regulations for food handlers and announcements that all water should be boiled before using. The
Raps included such helpful advice as not allowing dogs
to run at large or children to be around the swimming
hole unsupervised. At the front of the Information
Center were sign-up sheets for duty at the Kiddie
Meadow (also called Kiddieville) and the various kitchens, medical units, and other facilities. There was not, I
noted, any telephone, two-way radio, or other means of
communication as required by North Carolina's mass
gathering law. Ralph's co-worker was a young, smiling woman dressed in what appeared to be a buckskin
loin cloth. She also wore hand-tooled moccasins and
a feathered headdress. Her long, straight blonde hair
and creamy bosom contrasted strangely with the pseu-
do-Native American costume.

Indeed, I would note that while I saw many Rainbows
dressed in tribute to or imitation of American Indians,
only one of them actually appeared to be of that ethnic
stock. She was a woman who looked no more than
twenty, wearing a headband with a single feather and a
strangely shimmering, fringed two-piece dress of some
material I could not identify. It looked very expensive
and more like a costume from a 20th-century Wild
West show than anything you might really have found
on a reservation or in a pre-Columbian tribal camp.

But back to the blonde. When she saw Garrick she
shouted at him. "Garrick, where have you been? The

parade's already gone and the kiddie entertainment is going on over at the gypsy village. You'd better get over there. What if they need a story?"

"Garrick's a storyteller," Welcome Woman told me.

"I thought he seemed fairly honest," I replied.

She laughed, more than my remark deserved, and explained. "That's one of the things he does between gatherings to earn his living."

I was afraid to ask what else he did. Bob asked.

"He's a consultant," Welcome Woman said.

That's all we got out of them and that's all you'll get out of me.

Garrick, Welcome Woman, and Principle called Ralph (or whatever his name was) aside and we explained the purpose of the tour. Blonde Indian found a new assistant. Garrick rushed off, presumably to the Gypsy Meadow to tell one of his stories, if requested. (I'm told he tells them for free at the gatherings.) I suspect he also rushed about warning people that we were coming and why, but I never knew that for sure. It really didn't matter much. It was fairly obvious from the recently pressed appearance of our clothes that we were something other than just new arrivals at the Rainbow reunion. Throughout the tour, I saw people hastily ducking and disposing of cigarettes as we approached. By the time we reached any group, all smokes still in evidence looked and smelled to be tobacco, although many were handrolled. Often, however, the lingering odor in the air was not tobacco. But what you can't see may not be there.

Just past the Information Center stood two more pole-and-canvas structures. Each was roughly thirty feet long. They stood at right angles to each other, about forty feet apart. The guides led us to the one labeled "MASH UNIT." Two young women were on duty there. One was saying something about bug bites to a young man wearing only a leather vest as he held his penis up with one hand while she rubbed some sort of salve on his scrotum.

Principle introduced me. "This is Dave. He's having a tour and he needs to find out about the CALM unit and the MASH unit."

"Are you from the health department?" asked the young woman who was not attending the patient.

> C.A.L.M. / M.A.S.H.
> CENTER FOR ALTERNATIVE LIVING MEDICINE. IN THIS WOUNDED WORLD MANY OF OUR FAMILY COME TO THE GATHERING IN NEED OF HEALING. CALM PROVIDES FREE HEALTH CARE, HEALING WORKSHOPS, A WOMAN'S CENTER, AN HERBAL APOTHECARY, AND COUNSELING TO ALL IN NEED.
> LOOK FOR THE LARGE TENTS STAFFED WITH RAINBOW DOCTORS, NURSES AND OTHER MEDICINE PEOPLE, MASH PROVIDES FIELD CARE AND AN EVAC UNIT, WITH EMERGENCY SERVICES AND VOLUNTEER EXPERTS WHO COMBINE GENTLE NATURAL REMEDIES TO PROMOTE THE BODY'S OWN DEFENSES AND STANDARD MEDICAL PRACTICE.

"No," I said.

My "no" hung in the air. The young man in the vest took his salve and wandered away. The two young women stood looking up at me expecting some further explanation than simply "no." I gave none.

Ralph broke the silence. "Both these sisters," Rainbows often call each other brothers and sisters, "are registered nurses. Show him your credentials," he said to the first one he had introduced me to. At that point her credentials were about all she had that she was not showing me. The only things that I could see that connected her with nursing were the small, square white apron, brief white shorts, and white tennis shoes and socks which were all that she wore. Apparently this is enough to be a uniform at a Rainbow MASH unit. Her companion was wearing more clothes, in fact, a rather complete outfit, but no part of it resembled a nursing uniform, or at least I never saw an on-duty nurse in cutoff jeans and a "Welcome Home" T-shirt. However, each of them produced documents showing herself to be a registered nurse connected with a hospital in some other state.

"We do this every year during our vacation," one of them told me. "There are three other RNs here, and we sort of take turns. Other people help out. We've got salves and ointments as you saw but no drugs for internal consumption. We take temperatures and do first aid and if we see anything that seems to warrant it, we tell people to get out of the camp and go see a doctor."

"Do I gather that there is no doctor on duty?" I asked. (North Carolina's mass gathering law requires one.)

"There's a doctor here," the salve-rubber told me, "but he doesn't want anybody to know it unless there's an emergency. He's on vacation."

"Is he licensed in North Carolina?" Bob asked.

"West Virginia, I think," said one of the nurses.

Ralph made sort of a shushing gesture to her, "We don't recognize the power of the State to license anything about our gathering."

"The State does," said Bob.

I made a shushing gesture to Bob and we went on to the CALM unit.

"Here we have a couple of licensed chiropractors, and one naturopath," Welcome Woman told us.

"I didn't think North Carolina licensed naturopaths," Beth whispered to me.

"She didn't say the naturopath was licensed," I whispered back.

At the CALM unit they introduced me to a chiropractor. There were four massage tables under one end of the canvas awning. The chiropractor was rubbing a naked, fat man who lay on his stomach on one of the tables. A naked man and woman lay on two of the other massage tables apparently awaiting their appointments. Nobody keeps careful time at a world peace and healing gathering. The chiropractor interrupted the treatments long enough to show me his facilities and tell me a little about their use. Canvas curtains screened a rough ten-foot square at one end.

"This is where we do private examinations," he told me, pulling back a canvas flap to reveal a fifth table. By this time I was curious to know just what sort of examination it was that required privacy in light of what we'd seen so far, but I did not ask.

"In addition to the three professionals, we have several skilled masseuses and facilities for steam. One fellow helps out who studied with a Navajo medicine man. Over there, you see the yurt," he gestured toward a strange-looking little structure of vaguely Eastern appearance. "We invite the handicapped to stay there so it will be convenient for them." He smiled proudly.

As if on cue, a naked man in a wheelchair rolled around from the other side of the yurt.

I asked a few more questions and we continued the tour.

8 ⚕ WHO ARE THE RAINBOWS?

To reach any more of our projected stops, we needed to cross the Main Meadow. Back when we were approaching the camp, I promised, or at least suggested, that I would offer some further comments on the general and varied nature of the people in attendance when we reached the camp. Since the Main Meadow was filling with gathering attenders of general and varied appearance, this is as good a time as any. The main thing I can say about their appearance is that it was general and varied. As I've already mentioned and as you may recall from the late '60s and early '70s, the term "hippie" covers a myriad of people. As I had expected, we saw many men with beards and shoulder-length hair and many women, and a few men, with hair far below their shoulders. I had also expected, since this was billed as a "reunion," that most of those in attendance would be roughly in an age group ranging from slightly younger than my own forty-four years down to somewhere in the early to mid-thirties. I always thought I was about six to eighteen months older than the generation gap, so just enough time had passed to put old hippies in that projected range. In fact, quite a few, probably a majority, fit. But somewhere along the way, they had picked up "members" (if that's the right word) ranging on up into their fifties, sixties, and I would venture seventies. I also saw couples and individuals as young as early twenties and perhaps late teens.

Not surprisingly, many of the old hippies had acquired families by now and there were many children. More on the children later when we reach Kiddieville and beyond, but just one passing thought at this moment. I saw many children from around ten years old down to infants. I saw a few whom I would estimate at eleven or twelve. But, while I saw, as I said, a few detached individuals in their late teens, I saw no teenagers with family units. Since many of the Rainbows were my own age and beyond and since my own daughters were by then in or approaching their teens, I've given some thought to the reasons for this absence. I can think of two explanations, one or both of which may have some validity. I first thought that perhaps even old hippies, when their sons and daughters approach adolescence, may be either embarrassed or fearful about bringing them to a large gathering with so much open nudity, and, so it is rumored, free love, open sex, cheap drugs, and "alternative lifestyles."

In that connection, I later thought how interesting it might be to read the next September's essays on "How I Spent My Summer Vacation" by some of the third- and fourth- graders. "We went out and lived in the woods and ran around naked for a few weeks, and then came back home and got diarrhea so bad we thought we'd all die."

The other explanation is perhaps a bit more subtle. It may be that the teenage children of old hippies simply refuse to go to hippie happenings. While the Rainbow reunion may sound like the very sort of thing the teenage children of conventional middle-class and yuppie Americans would defy their parents to attend, the other side of the coin just could be that the teenage children of old hippies defy their parents and stay away. After all, I think most of us agree that how most hippies became hippies in the first place was in rebellion or reaction against the lifestyle and ideas of their conventional and conservative parents. Might not it also be true that this classic pattern of adolescent behavior in the case of the children of old hippies takes the form of reaction against unconventional lifestyles and radical ideas by the adoption of conventionality and conservatism? Therefore if the hippie remnant wants to extend radicalism into future generations, perhaps they owe it to their children to register Republican, join the Presbyterian Church, put on three-piece suits, and head for the country club dance.

But back to the variety among the adults. I hope I haven't given the idea that full or near nudity was the universal order of the day. It was not. In fact, to move ahead just a little ways, as we were leaving the encampment later, we stopped to talk with a Forest Service officer. She had been stationed at the Welcome Center all day and wore an expression combining elements of boredom, shock, and bewilderment. "How's it going?" Bob asked her.

"Do you know," she said, "that about one man in every 20 is naked? And about one woman in 40?"

"I don't think I counted," Kip said. "Does your figure include topless?"

"No," she answered. "I gave up counting that, but I think it's about one in 10 for both sexes. Excluding children. I guess most of them are naked."

I asked her one more. "I've seen a lot of women wearing nothing but those blue work shirts unbuttoned and a lot of times tied back. Are you counting them as naked?

"They're the worst of all." She said. "Naked can be casual, a shirt tied back is exhibitionism." Her mouth drew into a taut line.

She never told me if she had counted them or just why that was exhibitionism and nakedness wasn't. Don't misunderstand me, I'm not disagreeing with her, but I had thought there was a possibility they were simply keeping the sun off their shoulders and backs. Of course it's also possible, since most of the women were wearing tennis shoes, that they had plans to leave the camp and visit one of those diners that has a sign saying "shirts and shoes required." That's not likely, but it would be interesting.

I do not question the accuracy of her poll, given the area where she was stationed. Had she made the tour to the swimming hole or even spent more time in the Main Meadow, I think her nudity ratio would probably have doubled but probably not more than tripled. To put it shortly, the nudity was far from universal. In fact, I observed an odd phenomenon that I had seen among hippies fifteen to twenty years before. That is, many of the ones who wear clothes at all wear far more than are appropriate. Without beating the same horse too much, it was a very hot day. Many of the Rainbows were wearing several layers of clothing, including leathers, furs, and knit vests. I have no explanation for this. I do know, however, that after several days in the woods I would hate to be downwind from them.

In addition to the many varieties of traditional hippie (if there is such a thing as a "traditional hippie") styles, from cutoffs and T-shirts to fatigues and long peasant dresses to quasi-Indian and frontier attire, there were many other styles in evidence. Since the gathering is not controlled by any admission require- ments and since "membership" is completely undefined and open to anyone who decides to be a member of the Rainbow Family, it is inaccurate to say that all those in attendance were hippies. Of the estimated peak atten- dance of 15,000 to 17,000 on July 4, 1987, probably fully 5,000 to 7,000 were residents of Western North Caro- lina and surrounding areas who had never heard of the Rainbows until that summer. They had never been hip- pies or attended any sort of hippie gathering. They were simply the curious, or the mildly eccentric, who wanted to go out in the Nantahala National Forest where they hoped to see people running around naked, or even be seen running around naked themselves, or to have access to some cheap dope and cheap thrills unlike any- thing they'd ever had before. Walter Mittys, if you will, at last breaking into their dreams, or rebels without a nerve at last having a chance to at least watch what they hadn't dared to do at very little cost to themselves and their respectability.

There were also the aforementioned Hari Krishnas. And there were, unfortunately, bikers. With their motorcycles and their leather jackets, sometimes displaying their colors, radiating an aura of meanness and hostility, they seemed to me even more out of place in the "world peace and healing" gathering than they would have been in those peaceful forests under more normal circumstances. Where some of the curious came to buy dope, I suspect the bikers came to sell it, though I don't know if anyone has ever proved that.

We also thought we saw some Deadheads. That, of course, is not totally out of the question at a hippie reunion. These groupies, fans, and followers of the Grateful Dead seem to turn up anywhere and especially should be expected among others nostalgic for the same approximate period. Especially, we were not surprised, since we had heard the Grateful Dead were playing in nearby Tennessee around that same time. So after we had passed some young men in Grateful Dead T-shirts sitting around an expensive-looking, live-in vehicle bearing Grateful Dead signs, I commented to Mike about the Deadheads.

"Those weren't Deadheads," he said.

"Of course they were Deadheads," Melanie defended me. "They were covered with Grateful Dead regalia."

"They weren't Deadheads," Mike insisted. "Those were the Grateful Dead."

Whether or not Mike was right about the people we saw being the Grateful Dead themselves – and I'm told he was right – I stand by my statement that there were Deadheads at the gathering. Wherever the Grateful Dead went, there their loyalists followed.

One more type among the campers deserves separate comment. Back in the late '60s there used to be a definition joke going around. Hippies, we said, were people who dropped out of society, didn't believe in holding regular jobs, didn't bathe and get hair cuts as often as the rest of us, and thought that a lot of the laws shouldn't apply to them. We've always had people like that, we used to say, but until the hippie movement started, we just called them "bums."

This joke may have been unfair to a lot of people in the hippie movement, but it was not unfair to a lot of the Rainbow campers. Some portion of those present at the Rainbow festival were most appropriately described as "bums." I suppose the more polite term is "hobo," but however you chose to describe them, some of those in attendance had no particular devotion to a philosophy of world peace, environmental sanctity, or communing with nature. They were simply men – and I believe they were all men, at least I saw no women who I would put in this category – who knock around with no fixed address, no regular employment, bumming what they can to live on, and picking up odd jobs when necessary. You see them around the country, by ones and twos, often near freight yards or hitchhiking down interstates. You know them by their weathered appearance, their vacant eyes which rarely look into yours, and usually their consummate skill at rolling their own tobacco cigarettes. Naturally, when they learn of a gathering where nobody expects them to work for their keep, where there is free food at clean communal kitchens, ready access to abusable substances, and a no-cash barter system in place, they drift in.

As I learned a little later, even free clothing is available. Some of the Orthodox Rainbows told me that free clothing and other items of barterable value that can be lifted from unwatched campsites enter the barter economy through the hobo faction. Naturally, they drift in. Naturally, many had.

Other than these discernible types and the true gypsies about whom I learned little (that little I'll share with you later), the Rainbow campers were simply old hippies. Some of the old hippies pursue that lifestyle year round. Garrick tells stories and serves as a consultant. Some of them are artists, some musicians. Some, including a charming fellow called Badger who joined my guides later in the tour, farm – often in an organic way. Others make crafts and do odd jobs. Come June or maybe even May, they start drifting toward the site of that year's Rainbow gathering. Others, like the nurses I had met, descend to normalcy during most of the year. They work straight, even yuppie, jobs. (I actually saw Mercedes and BMWs parked along the road.) They apparently accumulate their leave, and revert to hippiedom once a year. I like to think that members of this subspecies of old hippies bring their own potty facilities to the gathering, either in live-in vehicles or tents, and retire to the common latrines only for emptying and ash covering – hopefully in the afternoon when the latrines seem to be least in use.

We saw all these types along with individuals who totally defied classification as we left the medical units and walked up the gentle slope of the Main Meadow on our way to Kiddieville.

9 ⚕ ON BARTER, BABIES & WHY RAINBOWS ARE NOT REALLY MULTI-COLORED

Before we came to Kiddieville, we saw a sign pointing up a broad trail to our left directing us to "BARTER MEADOW." Though it had little to do with our official purpose in holding the jury view, this title did arouse our curiosity, or at least Melanie's.

"What's Barter Meadow?" she asked our guides.

"Since we don't use money at our gatherings," Principle answered, "when people have things that other people may want, or want things that other people may have, they come to Barter Meadow and swap for them."

This brought out the prosecutor in Bob. "Like what

> **TRADE CIRCLE**
> THE MUTUAL EXCHANGE OF GIFTS IS ENCOURAGED. MONEY CHANGING IN THE TEMPLE IS NOT. CRAFTS-PEOPLE OFTEN SPREAD BLANKETS AND TRADE CRYSTALS, FEATHERS, AND HAND CARVED AMULETS.

things?" he asked.

Our guides smiled. "There's no drugs or sex or anything like that swapped at Barter Meadow," Principle insisted. "They're strictly off limits. Just T-shirts, crafts, buttons, bumper stickers, maybe some exotic foods. Come on, we'll show you."

Despite his readiness, I was a little reluctant. How certain could we be of the observance of an "off limits" rule among a group that professes to have no rules? If we went there and saw drugs, Bob would have to take action. Trouble would start. Somebody could get hurt. Like me, for instance. "We need to get to Kiddieville," I said.

"No problem," Welcome Woman told me. "Barter Meadow isn't much of a meadow. Mostly it's a wide trail that was here when we got here. That's the long way up to Kiddie Meadow, anyway."

We headed up the trail through Barter Meadow. Along the trail, we saw very little bartering of anything legal or illegal, but many Rainbows of all types were sitting, or more often sprawling, along either side of the trail. As we entered the widening path into the small clearing which apparently constituted Barter Meadow proper, I saw to one side a naked woman lolling back on her elbows, her legs spread wide, displaying, apparently proudly, the most pubic hair I've ever seen on one human being. Her head was turned away from us as we approached, while she talked to a slender girl who appeared to be in her late teens lolling beside her. The young girl was wearing a cut-off T-shirt, and underpants. She was the only adult I saw in the camp in underpants although many of the children – most of the ones who were not totally naked – were dressed in that style. As we came around the bend toward them, we could hear the young girl say, "Straights coming. Do you want to cover up?" She offered her a scarf.

Apparently, she didn't. She looked up at us, said a surly "welcome home," and turned back to the conversation. Beyond them we saw Rainbows with cardboard displays of political buttons, stacks of tie-dyed T-shirts, "Welcome Home" shirts, hats, various leather items, and a lot of roots and things I didn't recognize. Apparently Bob didn't recognize them either, at least as being illegal substances, and nobody took any action other than looking around. Again, though, we saw only a few barterers and many sprawlers. Principle apparently picked up on this.

"Most people just come to Barter Meadow to talk, and if they see something they want, they go back and get something to swap for it, unless they happen to have something with them that the swapper wants," he informed us. I thought of the proud display of pubes we just passed and did not pursue that line of inquiry. I am satisfied though that if the Rainbows had not barred money from their system of exchange, they could have set up toll booths at each end of the Barter Meadow, advertised it in the community at large and had a good start on paying for the next year's gathering. I don't mean from selling things, just charging admission to see it.

We walked on toward the Kiddie Meadow.

KIDS ARE A CENTRAL FOCUS OF THE GATHERING!

The trail from the bartering place opened into a lovely three- or four-acre grassy clearing. It was largely empty at the time of our visit for reasons that our guides explained later. Toward the upper end of the meadow, the far end as we entered, timbers had been arranged, bolted, and then tied in parallel "X" formations. Stout poles lay across the tops of the Xs. Like the joints of the Xs, they were firmly secured. Ropes hung from the poles to leather slings at the bottom. Each of the swings so constructed had its own parallel Xs. I examined the arrangements rather closely. Each leg of each X was well sunk into the earth and solidly secured. The ropes were thick and strong. All connections were well and apparently skillfully made. A woman sat in one of the three swings nursing a baby. I've seen much less-safe equipment at public parks around the country. As I watched the woman gently swing while she nursed, I thought of Bill Cosby's famous admonition to children: "Never play on anything you haven't seen an adult on first."

Other play equipment around the meadow was as strong, sound, and well-made. A dozen or so small children played about the meadow, attended by an approximately equal number of adults. One little girl about four was sobbing softly in the arms of a young woman in one of the ankle length, frontier-style, cotton dresses you often see on old hippies. That woman and two other adults were comforting the child. One of them was holding what appeared to be a tobacco poultice against the child's little brown bottom while they all said things to her about a bad ol' bee.

That little naked, bee-stung child prompts two specific observations about the Rainbows and their children. First, though she was caucasian and almost blonde haired, her skin was an even brown tan all over. A few of the other children and adults who we saw had the same all-over tans. Most did not. I assumed, therefore, that a few of the old hippies have either found homes where they can practice the open freedom of the human body year round (perhaps these are among the farmers) or they've located places shortly before annual gatherings where they can work on their all-over tans (perhaps these are among the rest-of-the-year straights who are successfully yuppie enough to own private sun decks or visit tanning booths). Among the adults and children without the all-over tans, we saw an awful lot of pink-to-bright-red skin, particularly on buns and breasts. That must have made for some real difficult sleeping.

These observations on skin prompt one more digression. Contrary to their name, Rainbows are mostly one color – white. I do not mean that Rainbows are simply majority white like the American population in general. Rainbows are overwhelmingly white. We saw a few Orientals, the aforementioned one apparent Native American and very, very few blacks. When you consider that the core of the Rainbow population is the old hippie movement, this may not be too surprising. The hippie movement of the late '60s and early '70s mainly arose on college campuses. For a well-known complex of economic and sociological reasons, college campuses in those days, even more than today, were largely white. This partly explains the white predominance in the hippie movement. Partly, but not entirely.

Again, given the socio-economic facts of American life in the relevant period, most of the black minority students on college campuses in those days were first-generation college students. They came to college from working class stock, as did I and many other white students. Hippies came mostly from upper-middle class and upper class backgrounds. For the most part, I and my working class fellows, whether white or black, did not gravitate in the direction of the hippie movement. You were little more likely to find black and working class white students in the hippie houses around college towns than you were to find them in the fraternity houses, and for some of the same reasons. Concededly, fraternities did not want us. Concededly, the hippies did. Most fraternities in those days barred blacks and did not recruit working class whites. Hippiedom, on the other hand, was open to anyone, and given their loudly espoused devotion to civil rights and equality, hippies especially welcomed blacks. But exclusivity was not the only bar to fraternities for students of working class background. Fraternities were expensive. There were initiation fees, dues, and housing and food costs higher than on-campus dorms.

Hippiedom, of course, had no formal dues. All the hippies called on you to do was, "tune in, turn on, and drop out." But what they wanted us to drop out of meant turning our backs on what we had seen our parents work for, hope for, and pray for all our lives. What they wanted us to drop out of meant forgetting all the weekend, summer, and part-time jobs that we ourselves had labored through to get where we were. We had worked for our education. We had seen our parents work for a living. I do not suggest that students of upper-middle class backgrounds do not have parents who work. But they have never seen their parents work for a living. Their parents, so far as they could discern, had a living made. Their parents worked for luxuries, for respectability, and for large estates. Our parents worked to put food on the table and then worked extra hours to try to accumulate enough that we could go to college and have a "better life." We working class students, black and white, would have been giving up all that we and our parents had worked for had we tuned in, turned on and dropped out. Therefore, we could not join hippiedom for one of the same reasons we could not join fraternities. The price of admission was simply too high.

But, back to the little girl. The other observation which the little girl prompts is that she was the only child I saw crying in the Rainbow camp, and she had just been stung by a bee. Whatever else it may do to small children to bring them to a hippie gathering in the woods and let them play naked for a few weeks, it does not make them unhappy. Whatever else I concluded about the camp, I'm convinced the children were happy, safe, and generally well looked after. (Except, of course, for the shigellosis.)

Six or eight of the children were grouped around a slender young woman in her early twenties who was on her knees on the ground thumping on what looked like a wooden xylophone.

"What is she doing?" Bob whispered.

"I think she is teaching them Orff," Beth told him.

"If I'd known taking Orff meant watching a naked woman that looks like her crawl around on the ground, I'd have signed up for it some time ago," Kip whispered. (Despite the openness of so many things, we tended to whisper to each other when we were talking about the hippies.)

"They probably didn't even have Orff when you were a kid," Melanie put in.

"I don't mean then," Kip said. "I mean now."

I don't know how much our guides heard of our whispered conversations, but they resumed their guiding duties. "Helping in the Kiddie Meadow is very popular," Welcome Woman said. "If I wasn't so into welcoming, I'd do a lot more of it myself. Musicians like her and crafts people teach them little classes. They don't make it work. It's more like little games."

Principle interrupted. "There are usually a lot more children here than this. There's an activity going on right now and most of them are over at the gypsy camp."

"Yes," Welcome Woman took over, "you just missed the parade. The gypsies had their apes and the Krishnas put their elephant in it. We didn't bring it through the Kiddie Meadow, because it's a pretty good walk, and a lot of the parents just wanted the littler ones to stay here. We can take you down there if you'd like."

"Oh, yes," Melanie said, "we'd like that."

I gave her a look designed to remind her that this was a jury view and not a pleasure excursion. "Let's look around here first. We need to know about the child care."

10 ❧ MORE ON HEALTH, HIPPIE CLOTHES & HANDSOME HIKERS

At the end of the meadow stood another hobo kitchen. It was one of the largest in the encampment, and had an L-shape instead of the usual rectangle. At one end they showed us a first aid unit, equipped with Band-Aids, thermometers, and various salves and ointments, commercial and herbal. The kitchen itself had the usual cooking facilities, non-perishable foods, and triple wash-rinse plastic buckets we had seen at other sites. It also had the same system of garbage disposal as all the other kitchens.

This garbage system consisted of several large plastic garbage bags, each bearing a color-coded tag. One color denoted paper; one, food and other biodegradables; another, aluminum; another, glass; still another, other recyclables. This system prevailed throughout the encampment, with the same color codes. I'm told one woman, a Rainbow regular, makes the tags up in advance for each year's gathering. The Rainbows place the garbage bags at all kitchen sites and various other locations throughout the camp. We saw little or no litter outside the garbage areas. However, we did at times see overflowing garbage bags despite the Rainbows' constant assurances to us that regular collection was made. The Rainbows and the Highway Patrol, with at least the acquiescence of the Forest Service officers, had worked out a pass system to let their garbage vehicles go in and out to take the waste to local dumps and recycling facilities.

As we watched the children, whenever one dropped any sort of litter on the ground, an adult picked it up and properly disposed of it. However, from around the age of four, the children all seemed to know the color codes themselves, or at least knew that litter goes in bags and not on the ground.

The water for the Kiddie Kitchen came from the usual black pipe. The tap bore the now-familiar sign "SPRING WATER – BOIL BEFORE USING." One of the several kitchen attendants was busily boiling as we inspected.

"The kiddie water isn't piped very far," Principle told me. "We opened a spring just above here."

"I've been wanting to see where you've opened a spring," I told him.

"Come on, let's go," he said motioning us to follow.

He led us through a thick growth of laurel and a stand of pines along a narrow new-looking path. I noticed that the path ran beside the black pipe, which lay along a shallow wet weather run-off. The hippies, like experienced mountain farmers, know that the presence of a wet weather run often – though not always

— marks the location of a wet weather spring at its head. Here the water table will be close to the surface of the ground, thus offering, even in drought times like those we were then experiencing, a good location for a shallow well, or, if you're lucky, a spring with just a little digging. When we reached the head of the run at that site, we found that the Rainbows had in fact dug out a spring. Plastic sheeting completely covered the spring, and a sign proclaimed, "DRINKING WATER SPRING – DO NOT UNCOVER." A second sign read, "NO CAMPING ABOVE THIS POINT – NO CAMPING WITHIN 50 YARDS OF SPRING."

"As you can see, we tap the springs off on top after we dig them out," said Principle. "We line them with rocks. The signs are to keep people from camping uphill or close enough to risk contamination."

The protection of drinking water was a reason I was there. "Since you've told me you have no rules, or leaders, what if somebody violates the sign?" I asked.

"We have a security committee that regularly checks around the springs," Principle answered. He gestured toward Ralph. "Ralph's on the security committee."

"But without formal rules or leaders," I asked, "how does this security committee enforce the signs?"

"Peer pressure," Ralph replied simply.

Ralph was about six feet tall. Although he was dressed in full length jeans and a T-shirt, I could see that the wiry muscles in his body were unmixed with fat. He was not in any sense heavily built, but would easily have gone 200 pounds. When one of the law clerks had commented on the smell of decaying vegetation in a damp place, he had noted that it reminded him of night patrols in Vietnam. He wore in a sheath at his side a heavy steel knife with a leather-gripped handle, an eight- or nine-inch blade, and curving steel stops between the two parts. He could well have carried it to hack off branches for kindling wood and certainly it could have chopped down even small saplings. Whatever his purpose in carrying the tool, I do not think he would have needed many peers to exert an awful lot of pressure.

Then they took us across a ridge downhill from the spring. There we found the latrine that served Kiddieville. "Of course we don't expect the little ones to come back up here to the latrine," said Welcome Woman. "You may have seen the little pots down near the first aid supplies. They just use them and the adults do the emptying. Of course the little toddlers just poop wherever they happen to be and one of the Kiddieville volunteers scoops it up from behind them."

"I guess that's one of the less pleasant parts of working Kiddieville," said Mike.

"Not really," Welcome Woman responded. "It beats changing diapers, and you don't have to figure out what to do with a messy one afterward. It's probably a lot like having a dog and a pooper-scooper in the city, except

I don't guess you run the dog down and wipe its butt with leaves afterwards."

"Can we go to the gypsy camp now?" asked Melanie.

"What do you say, Dave?" Principle asked me. "It's kind of your show."

Displaying, I guess, the kind of decisiveness you'd expect from a federal judge, I shrugged.

"It's about half-a-mile from here back to the dirt road," Welcome Woman said. "It's another, oh, I guess, mile-and-a-half or two down to the gypsy camp. But you can see a lot more about the reunion on the way."

I looked at the other straights who had come with me. "What do you say?" I asked them. "Are you up to it?"

It must have been well over 90 degrees by then. Although we had been in the shade a lot of the time, we had already walked a few miles, not even counting the extra walk I'd had to and from the swimming hole before I rejoined the group. Kip is a camper and hiker by avocation. He would have been up to many more miles. Melanie appeared to be on an adrenaline high. She was up to anything. Bob, though, is a short-legged, rotund man who hasn't had to meet a police department physical in a lot of years. However, he, Mike, and Beth are all between ten and twenty years younger than me. If I was up to another hike, they weren't about to admit that they weren't.

"You could learn a lot more about the encampment

that way," Mike said.

"Let's go," I said, and we followed our guides back through Kiddie Meadow and down another new-looking path to the dusty Forest Service road.

Shortly after we reached the road and began our trek, up and downhill, toward the gypsy camp, we crossed a bridge spanning a small stream. I believe it eventually wound around to join the larger creek and form the swimming hole. On the bank of the creek stood a sign pointing to our left reading, "SUPPLY KITCHEN."

As I was about to ask how that differed from the other kitchens, Welcome Woman suggested, "Come on, let's show him the Supply Kitchen."

We walked over to what at first appeared to be simply the largest of the hobo kitchens I'd seen that day. However, behind it were some sturdy, well-constructed shelves and boxes with such labels as "freeze dried," "assorted spices," "herbs," and so on. A young man with a clipboard in his hands and a pencil behind his ear sat on an orange crate under the canvas awning. Despite the fact that he wore only a pair of cutoff blue jeans, his posture and serious, business-like expression made him look for all the world like every good supply clerk I had ever seen. He greeted our guides by name, bid the rest of us a muttered "welcome home," and explained the function of his installation.

"People come in. They got food. They don't know where to keep their food. They don't know what kitchen to take it to. We got lots of kitchens. We got one kitchen serves alcohol. That's outside the welcome sign. We got one kitchen that specializes in whole grain bread. We got one that makes stir fried vegetables. One makes sweets, no refined sugar, of course. They bring it in. I keep a list of what we've got, who needs what. I send it out. 'Til I got somebody to come get it or take it out, I keep it here. Works. Works every year. Been doin' this the last five reunions. Don't know how they got along without me before that."

"Wonder what he does between gatherings?" I muttered to no one in particular as we started away.

"Runs somebody's parts warehouse," Bob guessed.

Principle looked at Ralph. They both smiled. "Notice how short his hair is? Some of us think he's career military. Just doesn't tell them much about us or us much about them."

"A lot of us are vets. The rest of us just had sense enough to get out," Ralph added.

Welcome Woman wasn't paying much attention to our conversation, she was too intent on guiding us. "And over there," she said, gesturing toward a bank at the junction of the Forest Service road and the path to the Supply Kitchen, "is the Clothing Supply."

Appropriately enough, we saw jeans, cut-offs, T-shirts, and other items of clothing lying in a fairly orderly, if not entirely clean, display on the grass.

"If somebody has clothes that they don't particularly

want, they can leave them there for whoever needs or wants them," she explained.

At that moment, as if on cue, a tall young man coming from the direction in which we were going, stopped at the Clothing Supply, stripped off the khaki shorts which were all he was wearing, shook them out, and laid them neatly among the other garments. He looked up at the two obviously straight young women in our group, grinned broadly (one might say leeringly) and walked away. Melanie looked back at him and grinned, equally broadly.

Beth looked at her watch, looked at the ground, and then looked straight ahead as we started on to the gypsy camp. When she looked straight ahead, she looked straight at the naked back of a young man who had just passed us. He was tall, well-formed, and built like a college athlete – not a weightlifter or football lineman – but a running back, or perhaps a basketball guard. His torso was nicely tanned, down to a sharp line at his waist. From there to his upper thighs, his neat tight buttocks displayed the sort of pink that would soon be turning red and would surely be giving him a hard time before the reunion was over.

When I said this young Apollo was naked I was exaggerating mildly. He in fact affected a fashion we saw on several of the younger Rainbow males. Just below his tan line, he wore a string or thong. In the middle of the front of the thong where it was knotted together and drooped down on his body, he had tied a leaf. Neither his leaf nor any of the others we saw actu- ally covered any part of his anatomy and, if anything, served to call attention to the parts which people normally might be expected to cover. I suppose it's possible that the originator of this fashion had a Biblical significance in mind, although figs are not among the leaf-bearing plants we have in the western mountains of North Carolina. I think it more likely that it began as some sort of joke and continued as some sort of fad.

Melanie whispered as he went by, "I think that's funny the way those guys wear a leaf."

"I think it's hilarious," Bob whispered back. "That's a poison oak leaf that guy's wearing."

"I didn't look that close," I whispered.

"I did," said Melanie.

11 ⚹ ON A SYMBOLIC SHOWER CURTAIN & A PLEASANT PACHYDERM

As we quickened our steps after the stop at the supply area, we kept even pace with the edenic young man ahead of us. We met quite a few Rainbows coming the other way, many of them with tired but happy looking children who apparently had enjoyed as much of the kiddie entertainment at the gypsy camp as they could stand. Occasionally we passed Rainbows going in our direction. The young man in front of us passed one pair. A little boy, of perhaps four years, was striding manfully along in nothing but his tennis shoes, holding to the hand of a young woman, presumably his mother, in one of the long pioneer dresses.

"Look at that boy's bottom," Beth whispered.

"I am," responded Melanie enthusiastically, her eyes still fixed on the leaf-wearing hiker. "But I'd call him a man."

"I mean the little boy," Beth explained. "He's got bug bites all over his buns. I can't believe parents would bring a kid out here for this to happen to."

"Aw, come on," Melanie protested as we drew even with them. "He'd have bug bites if they took him to the beach in a bathing suit."

"He wouldn't have bug bites where he does now," Beth whispered as we passed them and she looked back.

Most of the way down to the gypsy camp, campers, old school buses, and other live-in vehicles lined the road. I became increasingly convinced that the Highway Patrol's estimate of the number of Rainbows already encamped was low. It dawned on me that the State might be inclined at this point to maintain a deliberate underestimate. Bob is a good lawyer and I knew he would not falsify anything. I also suspect that he would, on matters of guess and estimate, advise his troopers to give themselves the benefit of the doubt. So long as the attendance was not obviously over 5,000, confrontation could be delayed at least until a court ruling was in place. I had no quarrel with that strategy.

After about a mile, we came to a section of the road where the right-hand shoulder dropped off rather too sharply to permit any vehicle to park on that side. We could see from well away that a shower curtain hung beside an elevated section of black plastic pipe. It was just an ordinary-size shower curtain. While it screened the area behind it from one side, 300 more degrees of view were completely open. A shower head protruded from the tap on the pipe. As we reached the curtain, I saw that it bore a sign reading "SYMBOLIC SHOWER CURTAIN." A wet young woman was standing behind the curtain just outside the spray of the shower lathering her hair with shampoo. As we drew closer, she took a bar of soap out of a plastic bag on the ground and rubbed it all over her body. Then we walked up. At the edge of the shower curtain, our guides stopped and Principle began to talk matter-of-factly.

"Look at this," he said, gesturing toward the young woman in the shower, "since you're interested in water use. This is our communal shower. You'll note that the soapy water runs down that steep bank. Come here." He led me near enough to the young woman that I could feel the spray against my face as she shook out her wet hair under the shower. It felt cool and pleasant – the spray did, I mean.

"You'll notice how the soapy water runs off," he said

as she began to rub the bar of soap across her body again. "At the bottom," he explained as she worked the suds into her crotch with one hand while soaping her breasts with the other, "the ground flattens out so that it's a gentle slope. From there it's several hundred yards to any surface water and the soap has a chance to dissipate, in fact, so far no water has made it to a stream on the surface."

Welcome Woman took up the lecture. "Lots of the live-in vehicles have some sort of bath facilities built in. We're careful about disposal of their water, too. If they have toilets, then they have to empty at the latrines." I was glad to learn that there were indeed pots at the ends of some rainbows. "If it's just wash-up facilities, they can put it with the dirty water. You may have seen the dirty water barrels around the kitchens and campsites. That's collected from dishwashing water and live-in showers. We keep it around where fires are for fire control. Even the State people think that's a good idea."

I knew that this was not perhaps totally sufficient to comply with the State's fire regulations, but certainly it was a good idea.

The bather turned off the cock at the shower head, coyly reached around the Symbolic Curtain to a towel on the roadway side. After briskly drying herself, she reached back around the curtain for her cut-off jeans and T-shirt. Only when fully dressed did she step outside the curtain and go on her way, the opposite way from the gypsy camp.

Melanie set a brisk pace until we caught back up with the rosy-cheeked hiker. We fell back into step a few feet behind him and continued in lock step with him until we neared the camp of the gypsies.

Now these were real gypsies. I do not recall ever having encountered identifiable real gypsies in person before. I have seen "gypsy fortune tellers" at traveling circuses and carnivals. I have seen gypsies in old movies and TV shows, but not real gypsies in person. For the most part, the real gypsies fairly well matched what I had expected. There was no multi-colored, horse-drawn car, but there were three similarly decorated old buses pulled into a broad parking area beside the dirt road. Mingling with the crowd were two trained apes on chains held by long-skirted young women wearing colorful head scarves. A dark-faced old man in a bright patterned shirt and shapeless old hat sat in a cane-bottomed chair at the corner of one of the buses apparently attending four more apes chained to the bus. As we came into view of them, we heard singing voices. Our guides quickened the pace and left the road to take a shortcut through a small patch of woods to the back-side of the gypsy camp where the entertainment was apparently going on.

This was away from the backside of the leaf-wearing hiker. Melanie stole one last glance, and hurried after us. But we abruptly halted our pace as several Hari

Krishnas, replete in their saffron robes, came charging through the woods with an elephant. Now, concededly, the elephant was small as elephants go. However, elephants go rather large. Two dogs barking at the elephant, or the Krishnas, strained against two hippie couples who held them back. "Let us pet her," the hippies were calling. "We'll hold the dogs."

"She does not like dogs," one of the Krishnas shot back across his shoulder as they hurried on their way.

I do not know how one tells an elephant's emotional disposition. Nonetheless, as I looked in that elephant's eyes, I had the sense that dogs or no dogs, she was very happy. I have lived in and around the southern Appalachian Mountains most of my life. I have seen many sights in the forests of those mountains. I saw many things in the camp of the Rainbows. But, as I later told those who had accompanied me that day, I think the most incongruous sight I ever saw was a half-dozen orange-robed young men, their heads shaved except for long tufts at the crown, running through the Nantahala National Forest with a happy, high-spirited elephant.

Granted, when I told them that, Mike took issue.

"With all due respect, Your Honor," he insisted, "the most incongruous sight anyone ever saw in the Nantahala National Forest was a federal judge with his complete entourage following some guy who was buck naked except for a piece of string and a leaf down the Forest Service road to the gypsy camp."

It's hard to argue with Mike on that point, but since I saw the latter sight only as a participant, I'll stick with the elephant.

12 ✴ ENTERTAINMENT, REST & RELAXATION (OF BODY & RULES)

After the elephant cleared through us, I asked the guides, "Does that mean the entertainment is over?" "No," said Welcome Woman. "The elephant was only one feature. The main event is music and dancing participation."

I wondered what she meant by that. As we neared, I found out. About four dozen Rainbows had joined hands in two concentric circles. They danced around to music produced by a small Reggae band while they and the other Rainbows present sang. They were singing to the tune of the Jimi Hendrix number, *Voodoo Chile*. Everywhere the original version says "voodoo chile" the Rainbows were inserting "Rainbow child." The person in apparent charge was a large black man, his long hair done up in dreadlocks, more appropriate to the Reggae band than the Jimi Hendrix tradition from which they borrowed the song. He stalked around, chewing on a large unlit cigar, leading the band, giving directions to the dancers, and generally, I suppose, making sure the entertainment was a success.

Among the Rainbows there may be some traditional

connection between musical entertainment and a lack of clothing. Like the slender percussionist at Kiddieville, the large Reggae man was totally naked. He finished convincing me that going naked in public at a Rainbow gathering is like running for President in society at large. Just because you decide to do it doesn't mean that anyone else wants to see you do it or that you have any particular qualifications for the job. He was a little over six feet tall, but not enough over to comfortably carry his bulk, which I would estimate conservatively at 280 pounds. None of it was muscle. Not to be too indelicate, but in all other respects he also appeared under-qualified for going naked in public. Indeed, had he not been a rather hairy man, with his fat swollen breasts the disinterested observer would need to have drawn very close to have conclusively determined his sex.

But if he was under-qualified for public nudity, the same was not true of everyone in the circles. Although the event was billed as "kiddie" entertainment, fully three-fourths of the people in the circles had not been kiddies for a number of years. Perhaps they were in the circles in order to assist the kiddies, but the ratio between adults and children suggested to me that this was more of an everybody entertainment than a kiddie one. I particularly noticed two of those entertaining themselves, and the rest of us. On approximately opposite sides of the outer circle were the two most attractive young female Rainbows I had seen all day – two of the most attractive young females I would be likely to see in the next several days. As I said, the song was a modification of *Voodoo Chile*. That song, as adapted for Rainbow children, includes lots of instructions like "jump up Rainbow child" and "get down Rainbow child." As if in a tribal version of "Hokie Pokie," the dancers were going through the commands as they danced around the circle. One of the two young beauties was wearing a blue work shirt, embroidered with daisies, peace symbols and various other markings. It was not tied back, like some I saw that day, but it was completely unbuttoned. Most of the time it covered very little more than her back, and during the more extreme movements, it covered only the very upper part of that. The other young woman was wearing only some sort of gossamer rag tied around her waist. It looked like a rough triangle torn from an old slip. Part of the time it covered part of one buttock.

Just as we arrived, the Reggae leader stopped his band for a moment of instruction. The dancers, of course, stopped as well. As chance would have it, I was looking directly at the girl in the work shirt when they stopped. (I will confess the odds were pretty good that I would have been staring at either her or the one in the triangular rag whenever they stopped.) She caught my eye. Without dropping her gaze, she reached down and scratched in approximately the same anatomic region that baseball players are prone to scratch when the TV camera fixes on them. At this moment, it occurred to me that we had been walking most of the last few hours on a hot day without sitting down. I decided it was time we had a rest, so I sat down on the grass near the circle and bid the others to do likewise. We rested for forty-five minutes. Though some dancers dropped in and out during the course of that time, the two young women were in as good shape as they looked, and they continued throughout.

The taking of this rest was not as voyeuristic as it may at first sound. Not only was I genuinely tired, but Bob appeared to be exhausted. Mike appeared to be worn out. While it's true that Kip rather looked like an old pack horse, not bursting with energy but fully ready to keep on going as long as command might require, and Melanie still looked totally ready for anything, even young Beth looked like she was quite ready for a rest. I will say that all of us might have been more refreshed if we had taken some refreshment. None of us did. Bob apparently thought it inconsistent to eat and drink when the safety of the food and water was precisely what he was questioning. I thought it singularly inappropriate for me to eat or drink when the safety of the food and water was a part of what I would be passing on. My law clerks scrupulously functioned as extensions of the court and followed my lead. As to Mike, I suspect he was not as sure of the physical purity of the provisions as he was of the legal purity of his cause.

Thus we all remained hot, thirsty, and hungry even as we rested.

So after our rest, I suggested we had probably seen about all we had come for (and perhaps a great deal more) and it might be a good idea to get back to the car and back to town. I did not mention in the presence of our guides that I wanted to get back to where we could buy at least a cold soft drink and a fast food hamburger. And so it was that as the sun was just beginning to touch the treetops behind the gypsy meadow, we turned our backs and started out of the Rainbow camp.

13 ⚭ BACK TOWARD NORMALCY

Going back to the welcome station, we did not retrack through any of the meadows, or revisit any of the kitchens or other facilities, but simply stuck to the dusty road. Although the shadows were beginning to grow longer, the day was still hot and we were still dry. The scenes had lost a little of their novelty. We saw mostly more of what we'd seen already – sometimes a great deal more. We could tell that the population had increased during our stay. I'm not going to venture a guess as to the actual number of Rainbows by then encamped, but the road was a little busier; the campsites within view of the road were a little more numerous; and the whole scene was a little more crowded, and a little busier than it had been when we first entered the camp of the Rainbows.

I know you may hear stories from people who have visited these camps about how they watched sexual intercourse going on in public. We did not see any. We almost did. As we came toward one fairly late model van, its back door standing wide open, we saw a young couple, both nude, engaged in what might euphemistically be described as vigorous embrace. More bluntly, it might be called foreplay. But as they were busily caressing each other, Welcome Woman stepped smartly ahead of us and closed the door. I think it noteworthy that the van was not only rather new, but also bore none of the signs, bumper stickers, or other characteristic modifications typical of the Orthodox Rainbow, or old hippie.

I guess I should note in this connection that we never followed the signs pointing to "BOOGEY MEADOW." No one ever invited us to Boogey Meadow. No one ever discussed what Boogey Meadow was. However, I assume that if Boogey Meadow is what I assumed it was, it was deliberately placed off the main thoroughfares and, as in certain bookstores and theaters in mainstream society, the patrons of Boogey Meadow were consenting adults who knew what they were consenting to.

Other than that, the most memorable event of the return trip – to me at least, I will not speak for the varying memories of the others – occurred when we were about halfway back. Somewhere not too far from the supply kitchen, a man in his early forties, wearing bib overalls and a flannel work shirt in spite of the heat of the day, sat on a stump playing a five-string banjo. A five-string banjo is no easy instrument and he was playing it exceptionally well. As he played, he and a few others sang bluegrass songs. I stopped and sang a few bars of *Fox on the Run* with them. Now I confess that I do not sing well. In fact, I hit the right note only as a blind hog finds an acorn – that's by chance and every now and then. But I did sing enthusiastically and I got all the words right. So far as I know, the banjo player had no idea who I was, but it was obvious that I was somebody straight who probably had some official position since three prominent Rainbows (leaders, if they had such an office) were leading me through the camp with five other straights who were treating me deferentially. He seemed as much pleased as surprised that I knew the kind of music that he played. Ralph introduced me as, "Dave, from around here."

"You know where there's any good music places around here?" he asked me.

"Yeah," I told him. "I go to Bill Stanley's Barbecue and Bluegrass over in Asheville."

Actually I do go to Bill Stanley's Barbecue and Bluegrass. I go there because the music is good, the barbecue is tolerable and the companionship is outstanding. There is very little chance of meeting any other lawyers there, and therefore the companionship is much preferable to what it might be at some more prestigious locations. Fortunately or unfortunately depending on your viewpoint, Bill Stanley's has acquired a reputation and now the crowds are large and the tourists are numerous. Apparently a couple of the people singing with the banjo player had heard of that reputation. They sneered. "It's a commercial place," said one of them. "You wouldn't be interested," he told the banjo player.

We bid each other good day and we started off. The banjo player told his singers he needed to find something to eat and started after us. He caught me just around the next bend and asked, "Do you suppose a good banjo player could pick up any work at Bill Stanley's?"

I told him I didn't know, and I thought as we went on that even talented hippies may need to rise above their principles when it comes to making a living between Rainbow gatherings.

The next most memorable event on the way back came beside a live-in vehicle of traditional old hippie decoration. The side of the van displayed a stylized marijuana leaf design. Its dozen stickers included "LEGALIZE NEARLY EVERYTHING." We tired straights were lagging just a bit behind our leaders at that point. Before we could see into the open side of the van, and presumably before its occupants could see us, one of them spoke to Principle.

"Hey brother, we got some great crystal for sale." Principle stiffened in his tracks. Ralph was equal to the occasion. He rushed to the van, saying loudly, "Maybe you can sell some of those quartz crystals to the people we're guiding through." He turned back to us, "These brothers sell quartz crystals they collect around the country. Why don't you brothers go get some of your stash and bring it over here?"

Neither I nor Bob had any doubt that the crystal originally referred to was crystal meth, a then-popular drug. Neither I nor Bob had any doubt that there was no way anyone would ever prove that, so we shook off the offer of crystal quartz and continued on.

Finally, we passed the van where I'd heard the loud electric music that morning. True to my guide's earlier prediction, peace reigned. Whether the relevant peer pressure was from nearby campers or Ralph-type security guards, I do not know, but I suspect the former since the occupants of the van were happily and peacefully talking with their neighbors.

At last we passed the Moondancers' meadow where the stage was now complete. A new sign read "CONCERT TONIGHT." It gave no further details.

We came to the Welcome Center and Bob's parked car.

14 ✵ DOWN & OUT

The shuttles were still running, coming up the hill full, and going down largely empty. Streams of hippies still walked up the road. Bob's car, normally a five-placer, has a built-in gun box so that it only seats four comfortably. Beth and Melanie became perhaps the first law clerks to any federal judge to take a slow two-mile ride in the laps of two lawyers, one of them the counsel for civil rights plaintiffs, the other, more than ever, a friend of the court. But then I guess I was the first federal judge to attend a hippie gathering in the course of my official duties. For better or worse, it was not the last such visit. More on that later.

Bob radioed ahead, had the shuttles held again, one at the top, one at the bottom, and we drove down through the gathering horde. We dropped the clerks at Melanie's car, made arrangements to meet them at the next fast food place, four miles back on the way toward Asheville, talked with the troopers a few minutes, and headed east.

When we got to the hamburger place, thirsty and hungry as we were, we first rushed for the restroom. We had noticed, repeatedly I might add, that Rainbows aren't particularly particular about where they urinate and in front of whom. Lawyers, however, are. Therefore, I speak advisedly when I say we rushed. Inside the restroom, a bearded, long-haired man in worn buckskins was filling water jugs at the sink. Another man had stripped to his shorts and was scrubbing up in front of the other sink. I thought then about a passage from one of the affidavits I'd read earlier. A Forest Service report from an earlier Rainbow reunion described local reaction. "The reaction of the business community was mixed. Many said, 'They spend money. Love to have them back.' Others complained, 'They used the restrooms to bathe in. Caused a lot of extra work.'"

I never got an accurate reading on the reaction of the Graham County, North Carolina, business community. I suspect, however, the ambiguous description from the earlier reunion was accurate there as well. Graham County is not a particularly prosperous area, though a nearby power company dam has created a lake popular with boaters in season, and the nearby hunting draws some customers, also in season. I understand the restaurants, filling stations, and grocery stores actually had the best June and July anyone could remember. One local merchant actually donated a used car to a drawing the Rainbows held to help defray general expenses of the gathering. On the other hand, I am quite certain that these strange new visitors didn't always leave the facilities as neat as local custom.

After a few minutes we went into the restaurant, ordered our burgers, and found a table big enough for six, where my law clerks joined us after their visit to the ladies' room.

You may not be surprised to learn that the table talk mostly concerned the Rainbow gathering. While it's true that judges and their clerks normally do not discuss pending cases with others outside of court, there is no impropriety when the attorneys for all sides are present. If the judge wishes, he may of course require everyone to wait until they are in the courtroom and on record. Perhaps normally, I would. However, since the entire nature of the excursion was as a jury view, and since that automatically presupposes something in the nature of a taking of evidence to be reduced to record later, I saw no harm. Besides, whatever you may have heard to the contrary, judges are human too. There was no way I was going to try to stop that group from talking about the gathering we had just left.

All three attorneys had made themselves rather knowledgeable about the Rainbow movement and the prior gatherings in advance. My law clerks exercised a certain curiosity.

"Don't the laws of North Carolina apply on the Forest Service land?" Beth asked Kip. She knew they did.

"Yes," Kip nodded. "That's the Assimilative Crimes Act." He looked upward, as lawyers do when they're recalling the text of a statute. "I don't remember how it's worded but essentially when a federal property is located within a state, the law of the state applies. On Forest Service property, we've achieved concurrent jurisdiction with the state, and either state officers can enforce state laws or federal officers can enforce federal laws or we can enforce each other's."

Beth looked perplexed. "Why then can't they arrest a few people for indecent exposure? Wouldn't that get the rest of them to put some clothes on?"

The three lawyers in the case shook their heads. Melanie said, "They're not hurting anybody."

Kip said, "That's not the way it works with Rainbows. Forest Service tried that at one gathering. There were about 7,000 or 8,000 hippies there. It wasn't as hot as it is today, and not more than 100 of them were naked. Service busted a dozen or so for indecent exposure. Within five minutes, there were 7,000 or 8,000 naked hippies in the national forest. I don't think we're going to try that this time."

I commented on how we had seen no alcohol at all in the Rainbow camp. "Didn't you see those guys with that ice chest full of beer at Shuttle Stop 2 on our way out?" Beth asked.

"No, and it's a good thing I didn't," I replied.

"You wouldn't have had somebody bust them would you, Judge?" Melanie asked.

"No," I replied. "As hot and thirsty as I was, if I'd seen a chest full of cold beer, I would have dragged its owner back to Barter Meadow and one of those hippies would soon have owned my hat, boots, and, possibly, the title to my Buick."

We talked a little more, compared notes on what we'd seen and what we hadn't, finished our burgers, and headed back toward Asheville.

Part III

Toward a Day
of Decision

15 ✤ A LESSON IN THE LAW –
THEORY OR PRACTICE?

Since I was riding in the car with the three attorneys for the three interested parties (or two interested parties and one interested *amicus*), I still felt free to discuss the case. On the way out I had read the file, the statutes, and the affidavits. Between inspecting latrines and getting out of the way of elephants, I had given some thought to the law.

"Bob," I asked our driver, "the obligations that this Mass Gatherings Act imposes, and the cost for extra law enforcement that it puts on, when the Republicans brought Reagan to North Carolina or the Democrats brought Mondale, did they have to pay any of those things?"

"No," he told me, "that only applies to gatherings of 5,000 or more lasting more than 24 hours in the outdoors."

"Does that give any First or Fourteenth Amendment problems?" I asked.

"No, it's a reasonable time, place, and manner restriction on the exercise of First Amendment rights," he argued. (States can impose reasonable time, place, and manner restrictions on First Amendment rights so long as they are not such as to abridge, restrict or "chill" the exercise of those rights.)

"It isn't either," Mike argued. "A presidential visit, a

candidate visit, lots of other political-type gatherings, generate the same kind of need for extra enforcement and precautions that a so-called mass gathering does. North Carolina only restricts the kind of gathering that less popular expressers hold, or I guess expressers of less popular viewpoints. Anyway, there's no principled distinction. It's an infringement of my clients' First Amendment rights to speech and assembly. You can't get around it, Judge," he insisted, "you've got to deny their restraining order against our gathering, and grant us restraint against enforcement of that unconstitutional law."

I turned to Mike. "Let me ask you a question," I told him. (I don't know why judges always say that to lawyers. There's no way they're going to try to stop a judge from asking them a question.) "Do I really have jurisdiction to do anything? I'm not sure this case is properly removed. I may not have subject matter jurisdiction."

There are two kinds of jurisdiction. Personal jurisdiction means that the person is properly before the court. Subject matter jurisdiction means the judge has the legal authority to act on a particular subject. It's this second kind that has always given us conservative lawyers and judges a lot of trouble with the decisions of many liberal jurists. When a judge acts outside his legal authority, I've always said, he's not much better than a vigilante. Granted, the "result-oriented judge" is seeking what he believes to be a just result. He's trying to do the "right" thing. But then so is the vigilante, or for that matter, the lynch mob. You don't ever hear lynch mobs in old western movies saying, "Let's go out and hang an innocent person."

"You know that under the *Pullman*-type abstention doctrine, federal courts are not supposed to act to invalidate a state law when there is a procedure for testing its constitutionality in the state court. You know that we're supposed to abstain until you've exhausted your state remedy," I lectured Mike.

"But Judge," he retorted, "the *Pullman* doctrine doesn't apply to emergencies."

"But you've created the emergency," I told him. "The State had a perfectly adequate and valid procedure for litigating this question in an ongoing lawsuit. You removed it to federal court. How can I hold *Pullman* doesn't apply in the face of that? Shouldn't I simply remand this to the state court where it was in the first place? Isn't this an improper removal?" Mike sat in silent dejection in the back seat. I turned back toward Bob. "Why are you so blasted quiet?" I asked him. "You haven't even moved for me to remand the case."

Bob looked straight ahead. He kept on driving. He smiled just a little. "No Judge, I haven't moved for a remand." He and Mike both looked a little sheepish. I'd seen that look before.

"Is someone going to enlighten me as to why there's been no motion for remand?" I asked.

"Judge," Bob said, "there's no way I'm going to be able to talk any state judge into hearing this case and deciding it before July 4th, let alone before the arrival of the 5,000th Rainbow, even if we knew which one was the 5,000th."

Kip was sitting on the right-hand side of the back seat directly behind me. He was just a little more smiling and a little less sheepish than the other attorneys, perhaps because he was only an *amicus curiae* and not a party to this conspiracy. He chimed in. "What are you going to do if the Judge remands it, Bob? Estimate 5,000 and tell your troopers to start arresting all of 'em for being in an illegal mass gathering? How many jail cells have you got vacant in Western North Carolina?"

"A lot less than 5,000," Bob said. "A whole lot less than 18,000 or 20,000 or however many thousand may finally show up. But I don't think we would have to arrest all of them. We'd just have the troopers tell 'em to disperse, and arrest the ones that didn't disperse. That would probably only mean we'd have to arrest nine or 10,000 outside, and that's only about a hundred times as many as we've got jail cells for, even if we had troopers enough to arrest them. Near as I can see unless the Judge solves this problem somehow, we're going to have to impose martial law and get the Governor to call up the National Guard."

I fully understood at this point why the attorneys had been rather reluctant to let me in on what had already passed between them. Subject matter jurisdiction is not like personal jurisdiction. If a judge doesn't have personal jurisdiction, the person in question can waive that defect. A party can agree to let the court have jurisdiction over him. The parties can by stipulation confer personal jurisdiction. But if the judge doesn't have subject matter jurisdiction, he's not supposed to act at all. He really should dismiss or remand the case *ex mero motu*. *Ex mero motu* is not the name of some famous ancient legal scholar. *Ex mero motu* is an old legal phrase that means "of its own motion." That is, the court should do it even if nobody asks the court to.

I didn't ask many more questions the rest of the way back to Asheville.

When I got back to my office, there was a message there that Casey had called me from New York. Casey is an old friend of mine from college days. We kept up with each other through the years because of our strong bond of personal affection, together with a mutual interest in conservative philosophy and, before my withdrawal into the judicial cloisters, Republican politics.

In those days, while I was awaiting Senate action on my nomination to the higher court, Casey checked with me from time to time to see how that was going. He was disturbed that Senator Kennedy and others were holding up my nomination and concerned that I might not be confirmed. I returned his call.

"Where have you been all day?" he asked me. "I called you about 10:30 this morning."

"You're not going to believe this, Casey, but I spent the day at a mass hippie gathering, it's called the Rainbow Reunion."

There was a long pause. Finally Casey replied, "I know you want to seek favor with the liberals, Sentelle, but this is ridiculous."

After a little more explanation, I went home, very tired, and went to bed.

16 ⚖ A HARD DAY'S NIGHT

Now the fact that I went home and went to bed, even coupled with the fact that I was very tired, does not mean that I went to sleep. No matter how I turned the day's events over and over in my mind, I kept coming back to the same questions. For a time I could get my mind to follow off after naked hippie dancers and running Krishna elephants. But try as I might, it would not follow them off into dreamland. Instead, my thoughts kept coming back to the questions of jurisdiction and constitutionality which this case presented.

On the one hand, I could find the State's statute to be unconstitutional. I hasten to say that I am not stating that it is, but it certainly had constitutional problems. If I declared it unconstitutional, the State could not stop the gathering, and its control would be limited to attempts to enforce State criminal laws. I knew without accepting Bob's count that there weren't enough jail cells or enough officers for all the hippies that would be violating North Carolina's indecent exposure statutes and drug laws. I feared that if the threat of the mass gathering law were taken off, the present *de facto* cease-fire might break down. In the present circumstances, troopers were at least controlling the bridge. Law and order was maintained along the highway. Anybody who went up that path knew where they were going, and the troopers were making it their business to warn any straight-looking visitors what they were getting into. Without the threat of the mass gathering law, the cooler heads in the camp might well lose control. As it was now, perhaps the inmates were running the asylum, but at least it was the most experienced, level-headed, peaceful of the inmates who were exercising the most peer pressure and keeping the asylum within at least invisible walls.

Even if that solution were a desirable one, should I impose it? I doubted my own jurisdiction. Under the *Pullman* abstention doctrine and various other rules of law, I questioned whether I should be acting at all. The Rainbows' proper remedy was either to have first applied for the permit and then sued to knock out its constitutionally questionable provisions, or to have let the State lawsuit run its course. Their proper remedy was not to blockade the achieving of a State remedy and do an end-run around the State courts to the federal jurisdiction. Constitutional litigation is not supposed to work that way. Should I then order a remand on my own motion, even in the face of the State's acquiescence, and send this back to the State courts where it should have stayed? A federal court's power comes from the Constitution and statutes passed pursuant thereto. It cannot be conferred by acquiescence of the parties.

But if I followed that course of action, the mass gathering law would remain in force, and Bob, or at least his elected superiors, might decide that there was little choice but to enforce it. They would not be able to. I suspected that there were already well over 5,000 in the camp. If there were not, there soon would be. How would the State or anyone else know when 5,000 got there? Even before the 5,000th arrived, the State's definition of a mass gathering included outdoor gatherings where it was "reasonably contemplated" 5,000 would gather. That threshold was met already. If Bob was really going to try to enforce this law by its terms, he could send his troopers in to order dispersal just as soon as I released my jurisdiction. When I signed a remand order my neighbor or some other gray-headed trooper could roll up into that camp with a bullhorn and say, "Disperse ye hippies," or whatever one says when one is attempting to disperse a mass gathering.

Finally, was I really doing what I should be doing by focusing on these results at all? A conservative judge, by

American definition, is one who is not result-oriented. He follows the letter of the law and the Constitution. He attempts to accomplish the intent of the framers of the Constitution or the legislative body that enacted the law. He does not seize jurisdiction to accomplish what he sees as a just and proper result. This does not mean, of course, that he avoids a just and proper result. Once he has determined the intent of the framers and determined that he has jurisdiction, then, at least in equitable actions, he tries to do the "right" thing. This time, however, I wasn't a bit sure that I had jurisdiction to do anything at all. I was certainly reluctant to strike down as unconstitutional a North Carolina statute which probably wasn't properly before me.

My mind chased around that circle like a jet in a holding pattern until finally, just before daybreak, I saw a place where I might be able to put down.

17 ⚬ A-COURTING WE WILL GO

I slept until my alarm radio roused me the next morning with the news that a local federal judge had spent the day before inspecting a hippie camp and that he would be holding a hearing this morning to determine whether or not that camp or any so conceived could long endure in the State of North Carolina. I went to my chambers just in time to review the papers in the case, call my law clerks together, don my robe and head for the courtroom.

Now usually when a judge is holding a non-jury, temporary restraining order hearing, he finds in the courtroom two lawyers, perhaps a witness or two, one or two litigants, and a lot of empty seats. Such was not the case that day. The courtroom was full. Other than a few reporters, most of the people in the spectator seats looked as if they had just stepped out of a time warp from 1969. Actually, that's not true. Most of them looked a good deal older than hippies looked in 1969. What they really looked like was the same crowd I'd seen at the Rainbow gathering the day before. None of them was naked – at least not yet. In fact all of them had shirts on. Garrick and half-a-dozen others had put on passable business suits, though I don't recall seeing any ties.

With those few modifications, the dress was just as I had left it at Nantahala National Forest. Oh yes, none of the Krishnas came, but a few of the bikers did; and I'm sure I recognized a hobo or two.

I had ordered the two principal attorneys to work out a stipulated description of what we had done the day before and what we had seen. Among the three of us, we managed to enter this stipulation into the record. (The stipulation dealt with water use, safety measures, health protection, and child care. It did not deal with personal descriptions of the people at the Rainbow reunion, their attire, or lack of the same. It did not get into many of the requirements of the North Carolina Mass Gathering law which were or were not complied with.)

Then the parties sought to introduce "live" evidence. That means, in addition to the affidavits that I had already read, they wanted me to hear some witnesses. The State presented a Forest Service officer who testified as to the number of cars along the road and how many average people he had seen get out of each car. I mentally questioned his terminology. I doubt he had seen any "average" people get out of any of the cars. I saw none in the camp. I believe he meant the average number of people he had seen get out of each car. In any event, he did that calculation and got 4,000 or so hippies into the camp. He didn't calculate in the large numbers riding in some of the live-in vehicles or the number of hitchhikers who didn't leave vehicles along the road at all. Therefore, I think his number was a gross underestimate.

By way of affidavit and live witness, the State told me how they expected a gathering of this magnitude in this confined an area of the forest to affect the compaction of the soil. We'd had some discussion of that at the fast food dinner table the night before. It was a lot more interesting there than it was in court.

At the table it went something like, "You put ten or fifteen thousand pairs of feet out there on that red clay dirt and it's going to pack it down like brick." That was

Kip's contribution.

"It'll be even worse if it rains," Bob added.

"It doesn't rain around here," Mike argued, "this drought's been going on so long the trout have fleas on them in Graham County." It was a lot less colorful in court, but the gist was the same. The Forest Service believed that if that many people gathered in that small an area, the clay would be compacted so hard that ordinary vegetation not only would be killed but would not regrow without bringing in heavy equipment to tear up the soil and recompact it before reseeding.

The witness also testified to several other things. He identified for the record maps of the Forest Service district where the present Rainbow gathering was going on and Forest Service records describing several of the previous sixteen reunions. At one point during the proceedings, Bob asked the witness about the nature of the Rainbow group itself. The following exchange ensued:

Q: To your knowledge, Officer McClung, what is the purpose of the Rainbow group now camped in the area of Bear Creek Hunter Shelter and Slick Rock Road?

MR. MOORE (MIKE): Objection.

THE COURT: Overruled for T.R.O. purposes.

A: From talking with various members and from reading that material, I guess I could best describe it as a meeting of nature lovers. They get together to meet with one another and communicate with nature. That seems to be it in a nutshell.

THE COURT: Do you withdraw your objection?

MR. MOORE (MIKE): Yes, sir, your Honor. Excuse me.

As that exchange illustrates, the hostilities were not always totally hostile.

Bob went on to question the witness about the proximity of the Rainbow gathering to the watershed of the little town of Tapoco. It seems that there are only two ridges separating that watershed from the area where the Rainbows were camping. Finally, Mike got his chance to cross-examine and the Court (that's me – when a judge says "the Court," he always means himself) asked a few questions. Between us, we were able to establish that the officer didn't really have any damned idea how many Rainbows were in the gathering.

Next, the State called as a witness an engineer from the North Carolina Division of Health Services. He testified that he had tested water from two sources on the site (one source was the spring near Kiddie Meadow) and that the water was unfit for human consumption. Mike's cross-examination of the witness established that he had tested only two of the numerous sources on site and that boiling for five minutes would kill the offending bacteria he found.

The witness also testified that he had met with the State health director prior to the bringing of the lawsuit and advised him of the facts as he saw them concerning the water. He also reestablished the fact attested by the first witness and evident from the Forest Service map that the Rainbow camp was awfully close to the Tapoco watershed and only two ridges away.

Finally, the State called the District sanitarian for the North Carolina Division of Health Services. He testified that he had served the encampment with a notice (delivered to a Mr. David Jacobs and several other people) that they needed to file an application for a mass gathering permit. He further testified that no such application had been filed. One by one, Bob asked the sanitarian about specific provisions of the mass gathering law. One by one, the sanitarian swore that no one on behalf of the Rainbows had submitted a plan for the limitation of the size of the crowd, a plan for security, a plan for the control of deaths, a plan for the prevention and control of fire, a plan for rapid evacuation, a certificate of responsibility from a physician licensed in the State of North Carolina for medical services at the area of the gathering, or a statement of responsibility for ambulance service by a licensed ambulance service operator. He further testified that on his last visit to the camp, several days before our visit, he had seen neither chemical toilets nor adequate dry covers on the latrines. He did not comment that there was no other cover of any sort.

The witness further established that there was

no refrigeration and no insect control, and that he observed animals present in a kitchen area. (He did not say what kind of animal. I presume he meant something other than human animals since one would expect their presence in a kitchen.)

The sanitarian also testified to difficulty in obtaining names and addresses of responsible persons as required by the mass gathering statute. After he testified about talking with a person who identified himself as "Mr. Gypsy Tripper," he swore that, "most of the names seem to be alien." No one pressed him for a definition of "alien."

With that the State rested.

Mike called his first witness, my old friend Garrick Beck. After establishing that Beck had been a member of the Rainbow family for 16 years and had attended 14 prior gatherings, Mike next directed Beck's testimony toward an attempt to take him and other individual Rainbows outside the terms of North Carolina's mass gathering statute. That statute is directed toward those who "organize, sponsor, or hold" a mass gathering. Garrick testified that he had not organized, sponsored, or held any of the gatherings. He simply was there as an individual assembling peacefully with his brothers and sisters. Each of the brothers and sisters was doing the same.

However, when Bob cross-examined Garrick, he established that Garrick had for many years maintained a post office box in the name of the Rainbow family in which he received the various "Raps," "Howdy Folks," and other mailings for circulation in his region, the northwestern United States. Since these mailings involved the call to assemble in the specific location of reunion, one might justifiably have concluded that he had something to do with holding and organizing the activity.

But, of course, this cross-examination did not come until after Mike had completed his direct examination of Garrick. Without attempting to establish that the Rainbows had complied with North Carolina's statute, Mike did walk Garrick through what they had actually done in terms of preventing erosion and fire, protecting the environment, and dealing with the other interests protected by the State law. Garrick told us about water-barring the trails, reseeding the meadows, and "naturalizing" all the area that the Rainbows had used. Indeed, he testified that they would leave it better than they had found it. He swore that they would improve wildlife habitation, and that after some of the other gatherings, they had actually pulled tons of metal out of the forests that had been discarded there over the decades before their gatherings. Rainbows considered these clean-up activities "environmentally educational" for their members.

These clean-up procedures would last for weeks after the gathering was actually over. The Rainbows would aerate the meadows with hand tools and reseed them with appropriate seeds. They would take the refuse from the camp (here, he told us about the color-coded divisions) to recycling centers. "Every piece of string tied to a tree will be removed," he promised.

"There is," Garrick testified, "a leaflet that circulates called 'Happy Trails' that educates people as to the process of leaving the site in as natural a condition as possible.

"Areas in camps that are used as show grounds are aerated and chopped up with hand tools in a specified manner. Leaves and dirt and twigs, sticks and rocks are scattered over this area. Loose brush is piled over these areas to encourage wildlife, insects, and other natural creatures to return to all of these areas."

I'm not sure he could have convinced all of the locals that encouraging insects was a terribly good idea, but we saw what he meant.

"All the fire pits have their rocks scattered. The ashes are put into the latrines and the pits are covered over with dirt on top of that and reseeded if necessary."

He went on in great detail about what would be a several week process of reclaiming the forest after the gathering had ended. He also told us about the community kitchens with a three-stage soapy water, bleach-disinfect, and hot rinse clean-up process. He told us that access to the kitchens themselves was controlled and the workers had to wash their hands. The

#701

Happy Trails

In preparation for leaving... Pack up all your trash & bring to the appropriate recycle areas. Dismantle & disappear your encampment. Vanish ALL traces. Firerocks scattered, ashes cold out & buried, pits filled in. Latrines & compost holes covered over. String & twine get removed from tree limbs. Hardened ground gets areated with tools for future root growth & moisture catch. All litter is picked up. Help with Recycling. Where everyone helps, the effort is easy.

When an area is clear & clean, then Naturalize! Scatter logs, branches, leaves, duff to disappear trails & camps and renew forest habitat. H_2O systems & latrine tops are removed & cleaned for next time. In Parking areas help with disabled vehicles and fully dismantle ramps & bridges. Steep places are water-barred to prevent erosion. The final crew reseeds appropriate seed to renew vegetation and complete the process.

Transport as many riders as possible to aid our travels. Treat local folks with great kindness. They have been kind to us.

Drive safely and share this Love wherever you go.

Rainbows maintained additional dish-washing facilities in the Main Meadow for people who brought their own dishes. The dirty water was partly used in fire control (about which he testified much more later) and the balance was disposed of in "water pits dug in the appropriate manner behind each kitchen."

As to fire control, in addition to the large buckets of water, hand tools for firefighting were maintained beside each community fire. Individual campsites did not have individual fires; only the common areas had fires. In the sixteen-year history of the Rainbows, they have never started a fire. The only fire at any of their gatherings occurred when lightning struck a cottonwood in New Mexico across a canyon from their gathering. The Rainbows fought that fire, according to Garrick, with a 500-person bucket brigade that greatly impressed the Forest Service.

Mike also used this witness to introduce a couple of exhibits. Now let me note what I mean by introducing exhibits. If you are accustomed to watching trial law shows on television, such as *Matlock* or *Perry Mason*, you've seen lawyers jump up, produce a piece of paper, and say something like, "This is a letter from the murder victim to his wife the day before he was killed."

It ain't like that in real life. How would we know the exhibit is what the lawyer says it is? Not that lawyers would lie (perish the thought), but just in case one of them might make a mistake, the law requires that a witness who professes actual knowledge of what an exhibit is swear that the exhibit is what it purports to be. Of course, the possibility always exists of a witness lying under oath, but the other side at least can cross-examine the witness and, hopefully, ferret out any such perjury for the court.

In this case, Garrick identified for us "Rap #107." This particular "Rap" contained brief instructions on first-aid facilities and environmental protection. It began with the general admonition, "PLEASE PROTECT THIS BEAUTIFUL LAND." It told the camper to use only "USE ONLY DOWN, DEAD WOOD." It informed the camper of the CALM – MASH units, the coded trash collection system, and the discouragement of alcohol, and insisted upon the packing of all trash and bringing it to collection points. "Rap #107" was a terse, short, directly worded advisory on campers and the environment. No one could get much more advice onto a 5" x 8" piece of paper than the Rainbows got onto "Rap #107." According to Garrick, the Rainbows made an effort to put a copy of "107" into the hands of every camper.

Garrick went on to testify about the health facilities, the various health professionals on site, and the borrowing of the latrine design from the Marines. (He made no mention of when or how the Rainbows decided not to borrow the canvas drapery as well.)

When Bob cross-examined Garrick, in addition to covering his "organizational" or "leadership" role as I

#107

GATHERING CONSCIOUSNESS

PLEASE PROTECT THIS BEAUTIFUL LAND. WALK
SOFTLY. Allow plants & animals to be. HARMONIZED ♫
BLENDIN≋. USE ONLY DOWN, DEAD WOOD. PRESERVE
THE MEADOWS... CAMP IN THE WOODS.

EVERYONE SHARING MAKES A STRONG HUMAN TRIBE!
PLEASE PROTECT THE WATER SOURCES, STAY OUT OF
DELICATE SPRING AREAS, PLEASE. AVOID CAMPING,
PEEING, WASHING ABOVE SPRING AREAS. KEEP ALL SOAP
OUT OF STREAMS, SPRINGS OR THE LAKE!
USE THE SLIT TRENCHES OR COVERED LATRINES, COVER
YOUR PAPER & WASTE WITH ASHES/LIME... WASH HANDS.
CAMP TOGETHER~ESTABLISH NEIGHBORHOODS.
COMMUNITY FIRES ONLY!~EACH WITH WATER BUCKET,
SHOVEL AND AX OR SAW FOR FIRE PROTECTION. WATCH YOUR
GEAR~"TEMPT NOT LEST YE BE LIFTED FROM." BE RESPONSIBLE
FOR YOUR ANIMALS. KEEP THEM FED AND OUT OF THE KITCHENS &
SPRINGS. LOVE THEM. SEPARATE GARBAGE FOR RECYCLING.
FIND NEAREST COLLECTION POINT. COMPOST IN PITS ONLY.
USE YOUR OWN BOWL & SPOON! PARTICIPATE IN ALL
ACTIVITIES, COUNCILS, WORK CREWS, WORKSHOPS. YOU ARE
THE GATHERING! R-E-S-P-E-C-T YOUR SISTERS &
BROTHERS ENERGIES. HEALTH PROBLEMS? CONTACT
C.A.L.M./M.A.S.H. FOR AID!
NOTICE THE BALANCE: EARTH, SKY, TREES, WATER & PEOPLE!
ALCOHOL IS DISCOURAGED, GUNS ARE INAPPROPRIATE.
DONATIONS TO THE MAGIC HAT FUND OUR NEEDS.
JOIN US FOR JULY 4TH SILENT CONTEMPLATION & PRAYER
FOR PEACE...

WE ♡ YOU

TO BE CERTAIN OF DRINKING WATER: BOIL IT!

mentioned before, he also questioned him about the lack of any attempt by the Rainbows to obtain a permit for the gathering. He in fact had Garrick identify another one-page Rainbow circular, a "Howdy Folks," which advised the reader to ignore all attempts to cancel the gathering: IGNORE ALL RUMORS OF CANCELLATION!

At this point, the Court (that's me again) asked him a few questions on that score. No, he admitted, the Rainbows had not made any attempt to comply with North Carolina's mass gathering law or to find out if North Carolina had any permit laws about mass gatherings. Yes, the approximate location of the 1987 reunion had been established in July of 1986, but, he defended, they had not known at that time whether the gathering would be in Georgia, Tennessee, Virginia, North Carolina or Kentucky. But, he admitted, they had made no inquiry as to the laws in any of those states either.

When all the questions were either answered or evaded, Garrick retreated from the witness stand to rejoin the audience, his head no more than slightly bloodied and not even slightly bowed.

Mike's second, third, and fourth witnesses were a little surprising. Until he was called to be sworn, I had supposed the second witness to be a newspaper reporter. He wore a business suit, white shirt, and tie. He was clean. His hair was shorter than mine and neatly combed. All in all, he looked a bit too respectable to be a newspaper reporter, but he looked more like one of them than one of the Rainbows. As his testimony developed, he was neither. He was an insurance agent who, so far as I know, had never attended any Rainbow reunions. His testimony was that obtaining the bond required by North Carolina's mass gathering statute for a Rainbow reunion was impossible. He did allow on cross-examination that a major bond writing company might write a bond of $1,000,000 for the Rainbows if the Rainbows put up $1,000,000 in escrow and paid a fee on top of that. Garrick had testified that general Rainbow expenses, such as the rent for Garrick's mail-drop post office box, were paid for out of a "magic hat." The hat, it seems, passes around through the camp and comes back with money in it. To the wonderment of none, the hat has never produced a million dollars.

Mike's third witness did not look as surprising as the second. He was a bit old for an old hippie. It was established during his cross-examination that he was then 58 years old. Other than his age, he looked much like what I would call a weekend hippie. His hair was a little long, but not outlandish. It was cut, but not recently. He had facial hair, but it was clean and neatly trimmed. His clothes were khakis, but decent and clean. I therefore suspected that he was one of those Rainbows who go straight forty-odd weeks of the year and go hip during an accumulated vacation of ten or twelve very odd weeks.

I was approximately correct. Witness No. 3 was a

biologist with a bachelor's degree from the University of Connecticut and a master's from Yale University. While employed at the time of the hearing as a manager of a recycling center in New Hampshire, he had for many years taught biology at the university level and in private schools. He had left Yale in the early '70s. He had attended several Rainbow reunions. I surmised, though the evidence was certainly not explicit, that he might have gone back to graduate school after some years of teaching, there fallen in with the hippie movement, and then had a wonderful time. It happens. In fact, some Rainbows told me that I was not the first judge ever to attend one of their gatherings. Some years before, they claimed, a local judge in a town near a Rainbow gathering came to observe and stayed to join. They tell me he never held another day of court but now drives something called the "Green Turtle Bus" and attends all Rainbow gatherings.

Whether or not there is any truth to the legend of the Green Turtle Judge, the Yale-educated recycling biologist was real and was in my court. He testified that the Rainbows took good care of the water and that there was plenty of water there for a half-million people, if they boiled it first. By his account, the Rainbow gathering was less a threat to the environment than anywhere else he had ever seen with that many people. He thought towns should emulate the Rainbows in their use and handling of water.

He did testify that he had not examined the communal shower. (Of course I had, but then I'm not a water expert.) He testified he took his shower (with biodegradable soap) at another location about 150 yards from one of the mountain streams. He didn't say where he went to the potty. I note also that he did say that he took his "shower" not "showers." I'm just as glad that I did not get downwind of him.

If the third witness and his background surprised me a bit, the fourth surprised me more. He was Dr. William Smith. Dr. Smith's age did not come into evidence, but he had held his Ph.D. in geology for over twenty years and appeared to be well over sixty years old. Both his beard and hair were white and they, like his general appearance, well fit the adjective "scraggly." He presented a curriculum vitae for qualification as an expert witness that included authorship of over a dozen scholarly publications. If the third witness had followed off after the hippies in the 1960s, the fourth had followed them a lot further. He was no longer teaching and described his present work as a "freelance consultant in environmental sciences and environmental planning." He was a resident of Baton Rouge, Louisiana, but stated that, "at the present time, I have no particular apartment or house there that I use." For purposes of the Rainbow gatherings, he was a resident ecologist. He assisted in the finding and opening of springs. He advised on locations for kitchens and latrines. He saw to the protection of watersheds. Nothing in the Tapoco watershed was downhill from anything in the Rainbow camp which could contaminate it. There was a ridge or two between them. He saw no danger of contamination.

At last, in a lot more time than it takes to tell about it, both sides rested. It was almost the time of decision.

I let the lawyers argue, a little, and then the Court spoke.

18 ⚜ STATE V. THE HIPPIES

Before getting to what the Court (that's me, remember) had to say, I would note that the evidence in court on this particular conflict reflects on a much greater conflict. Briefly reviewed, the history of the hippie movement is a history of conflict between people of that philosophy and the state. In our case in court, the State's evidence and that of the Rainbows never really contradicted each other at all. Rather the two sets of witnesses testified past each other. They were like trains heading toward each other but never colliding because they were on parallel tracks, not the same one. While they did not collide, neither did they engage. The State and the hippies simply were not talking about the same thing. The State's witnesses testified that the Rainbows were not in compliance with the State's laws. The Rainbows did not deny that. Rather, they offered evidence that their way was at least as good as the State's and maybe better. This, I think, is what happened to the hippie movement. While it might be said that the hippie movement was too amorphous to have a center, the closest to a center it came was a world view of each one doing one's own thing. If the state said to do a certain act or to do an act in a certain way, and an individual felt that he or she had derived a better thing to do or a better way to do a thing, then the individual's thing was the thing the individual did.

For a time, this notion had a certain allure for a lot of people – particularly for those who were young enough to be idealistic enough to think that all people would act for the greater good if simply given the freedom to do so. However, most people realized from the start that not all people are well-meaning and that even well-meaning people can disagree. Most of those who did not realize this at the beginning found it out with the passage of time and the rudeness of experiencing reality. Most realized that through history man has developed institutions, often embodied in the state, for imposing an order upon the chaos that results from a mass of people acting on a mass of impulses and opinions. Where there has been no such institution, the strongest have prevailed. In order to preserve a society with sufficient freedom for each individual to have some chance of achieving his individual goals, there must be an institution with some power to pursue the collective goals. For that institution to protect the weak from the strong and the few from the many, it must itself have the strength to pursue the collective goals in those limited areas taken away from the individuals. The hippies of the '60s and early '70s kicked against the walls of society. To a limited extent, they broke free. Perhaps they showed us places where those walls needed to be broken or pushed further apart. But as a general proposition, they mostly succeeded in demonstrating to the rest of society what the less-intellectual had intuitively known all along. The only real liberty is an ordered liberty. An anarchy without some general rules cannot in the long run provide for the weak, protect the unpopular or maintain any real protection for anyone.

The conflict in the Nantahala Forest presented a microcosmic section of that cosmic debate. The State had decided how the health and welfare of the people were to be protected. Perhaps it had done so wrongly. But did that in and of itself give a few thousand people the right to substitute their vision for the product of the common experience of millions?

In fairness though to the hippies, if the state is to properly perform its office, it must remember that, at least in our western tradition, that proper office concerns the preservation of order and liberty, not simply the preservation of order. Our governments, particularly in the United States, function only within the bounds of constitutional strictures designed and evolved for the purpose of ensuring that the state does not overstep the role of common protector to assume the role of common dictator. Had North Carolina here stepped over those constitutional walls?

None of this answers my question as to what the Court should do or answers your question as to what the Court did do. As my mind had circled the questions the night before, as I grew more and more confused and sleepy, I thought about one of the men who had preceded me as district judge for the Western District of North Carolina. His name was Wilson Warlick, but rarely did anyone call him that. In court, you called him "Your Honor." Out of court, to his face, you called him "Your Honor," or "Judge." When you talked about him, you affectionately called him "Coot." Coot was short for "Cooter," a name his nanny had given him when he was one year old because, according to her, he crawled like a "cooter" – a country slang for turtle or terrapin. "Coot" he'd been for well over seventy years when I first met him and "Coot" he was the day he died in his late eighties after over forty years of holding court as first a state then a federal judge.

Coot still held court actively in his seventies and eighties. He had not stayed entirely current in legal scholarship and, in fact, often said he had little use for some of the newfangled ideas that came down from the appellate courts. But what he may have lacked in current scholarship, he more than made up for in experience and wisdom. Certainly he made mistakes – sometimes prejudicial ones. Certainly he suffered from biases – sometimes sadly so. But all-in-all, he tried to do the right thing and to be the best judge he could according to the light that he had. Sometime in the later hours of my sleeplessness, I asked myself the question, "What would Coot do?"

I could almost hear him say, "Sentelle, it ain't that hard, my boy." He always called me "my boy." I found that in no sense demeaning since he always called his friend U. S. Senator Sam J. Ervin, Jr. of Watergate fame "young Sam," even after the Senator's father had been dead for decades.

"Sentelle," he would have said, "what those hippies want is to have their party. What the State of North Carolina wants to do is look after the Tapoco watershed and try to keep those hippies from making any more folks sick around the camp than what's gonna get sick anyway. Now you just forget 'bout all your high falutin' theories for a minute and take the common sense that God gave you back into chambers with those two lawyers and beat their heads together 'til they consent to something that accomplishes all those goals."

That was just about what I did.

I spoke first to the State of North Carolina. "I see three things that the State is attempting to accomplish here. The first one is to protect the health of the citizens of North Carolina, more specifically the watershed of

e second thing is to protect the health of
on the site of the Rainbow gathering. The
vindicate the authority of the State of North
to maintain and establish the validity of this
statutory scheme for future mass gatherings.

"But," I said, "the order which I can grant on the
pleadings and the law in front of me will not accomplish any of these results. The statute has constitutional
problems. These were not properly raised before me.
Entering this order will not provide any precedent to
accomplish the State's third goal. Any future mass gathering will still raise the constitutional questions anew
because they were not properly raised here.

"Even if I enter the orders the State asks me to enter,
am I really accomplishing goals 1 and 2?" I suggested
I was not. If we entered a mandatory injunction order
limiting that gathering to 5,000, I did not see how it
could apply until 5,000 were actually there. Then under
the terms of the statute, it would relate back to the
beginning of the gathering and everybody could theo-
retically be run out. But how did we know when 5,000
got there and how much more would 5,001 endan-
ger the watershed of Tapoco or the well-being of the
citizens than would 4,999? If the State really wants to
protect health and welfare, then it needs a mechanism
better designed for that purpose than an order restraining the gathering of 5,000 or more persons.

To the Rainbows and their counsel I said, "What is

it that you really want?" I suggested that the Rainbows did not really have a primary goal of striking down the law that threatened to interfere with their gathering. Their primary goal was to have their gathering. They had a means to test the constitutionality of the statute. Whether by accident or design they had made no attempt to comply and had sandbagged the State on the constitutionality question. Therefore, I told them I would be perfectly justified in not listening to their constitutional arguments, treating the statute as constitutional for purposes of this case, and entering the order for which the State prayed. On the other hand, I told the State that if I decided to remand this case or to enter the order the Rainbows sought, where would the State be then?

"Right now," I said, "there are no Rainbow facilities draining into Tapoco's watershed. There's at least one, and it appears from the topographical maps two, ridges between any part of that watershed and any Rainbow water use. What you really want is the imposition of health regulations. What the Rainbows really want is to have their gathering. I cannot enter an order that provides either of these results. However, the parties can do by consent what the court cannot do by coercion. Therefore, I now suggest that I retire with counsel to my chambers to attempt to achieve a consent order agreeable to all parties."

19 ✳ THE AGE OF CONSENT

Unless you have at some time in your experience participated in a conference attempting to achieve a consent judgment, you have no idea how bad one of them is. I had always supposed that the worst such settlement conferences were those involving domestic disputes. As a matter of fact, I still suppose that. When I was a state judge involved with domestic law, I saw settlement conferences fall apart over such vital questions as which spouse got the newest blender and who should have the antique china cabinet key. Mind you, the family did not own an antique china cabinet, it was simply a key. Domestic conferences are the worst. But the next to the worst type of settlement conference I now know to be a settlement conference involving litigation over a hippie reunion. After a several-hour conference involving the Court (that's me, remember), the State's attorney, and the ACLU lawyer representing the Rainbows, we finally reached a twenty-three-paragraph, four-page consent judgment by agreement.

That sounds simple enough, except that each paragraph of the agreement involved first, a dispute between the attorneys; second, a pushing toward resolution by the Court; third, each attorney conferring with clients or superiors (Mike in the hallway, Bob by telephone); and finally a repeat of steps 1, 2 and 3 after the first conference with clients produced changes in the then-current version. Sometimes we went through two or three more repetitions. In the end, we produced the following agreement (plaintiff being Dr. Ronald H. Levine for the State Health Department and defendants being the Rainbows, individually and collectively):

AGREEMENT:

1. The defendants herein will immediately use only boiled water for human consumption.

2. The defendants herein will immediately use only chlorinated water in cleaning pots, pans, utensils, and dishes used for the preparation and consumption of food for human use.

3. The defendants herein will submit a set of specifications for construction of latrines to a designated representative of the plaintiff within twenty-four (24) hours after entry of this Order. In the event of failure to submit such specifications, or in the event said specifications are unacceptable to the designated representatives of the plaintiff, the standards set forth in the current Marine Corps field manual shall apply. Construction of latrines shall comply with said standards.

4. The defendants herein shall cover all human waste with dirt, ashes, lime or a combination of said materials immediately after use.

5. The defendants herein shall identify the head of any developed water sources, shall mark off an area around any developed water source, and entry into said area by persons or animals shall be prohibited.

6. The defendants herein shall post in all latrine areas signs noting that food handlers are required to wash hands and at all kitchens and water sources signs requiring the boiling of water for human consumption.

7. The defendants herein shall monitor or cause to be monitored open water, water supplies, or water sources to prohibit contamination with human excrement.

8. The defendants herein shall not block forest Development Road No. 62 (also known as Slick Rock Road) to use for emergency evacuation or to use by emergency vehicles for any purpose, including ambulance, fire, law enforcement, and public health vehicles.

9. The defendants herein shall store or cause to be stored all solid waste material in a manner so as to prevent exposure to insects and animals and said material shall be removed and disposed of in containers provided at the entrance to Slick Rock Road daily.

10. The defendants herein do hereby indicate their understanding that the laws of North Carolina concerning impairing substances will be enforced by appropriate authorities as by law provided.

11. The defendants herein do hereby indicate their understanding that no individual shall resist, delay, or obstruct the monitoring of this agreement by State or local public health officers.

12. The defendants herein indicate their understanding that any person found within the designated boundaries of the Tapoco Watershed shall be subject to immediate arrest by virtue of 10 N.C.A.C. 10A.1201 as incorporated within N.C.G.S. § 130A-25.

13. The defendants herein shall clear or cause to be cleared an area of not less than three feet of any flammable materials around any fire.

14. The defendants herein shall locate or cause to be located a container of water and a container of dirt at the site of any fire for the purpose of extinguishing any fire outbreak.

15. The defendants herein shall identify a physician licensed in North Carolina who is willing to confer in the development and implementation of a plan for providing necessary medical services to the designated representative of the Division of Health Services.

16. The defendants herein shall post a sign at the entrance to Forest Development Road No. 62 or Slick Rock Road which shall contain in a clearly visible and eye catching manner the following:

"CAUTION – NORTH CAROLINA LAW REQUIRES
A PERMIT FOR A MASS GATHERING
OF MORE THAN 5,000 PEOPLE.
NO SUCH PERMIT HAS BEEN OBTAINED."

17. The promises contained in paragraphs 5, 6, 12, 13, and 15 set forth above shall be completed within 24 hours after the entry of this order.

18. The plaintiff shall designate a person or persons who shall monitor the site of the Rainbow Gath-

ering for substantial compliance with the promises set forth above.

19. The plaintiff waives any and all right to pursue monetary damages against the defendants herein by virtue of N.C.G.S. § 130A-254(e).

20. Both plaintiff and defendants herein agree that a liaison committee consisting of the named defendants, Garrick Beck and Stephen M. Sedlacko [a.k.a. "Principle"], as representatives of the Rainbow Family, and a representative designated by the plaintiff shall confer on issues relating to this agreement. Officials of local and federal government shall be extended an invitation to participate in the discussion of this committee.

21. If the promises of the defendants herein are substantially complied with and no sufficient evidence indicates that more than 5,000 people were present at the site of the Rainbow Gathering in any twenty-four hour period then the plaintiff shall file a notice of voluntary dismissal with prejudice.

22. Both plaintiff and defendants herein contemplate and agree that any substantial violation of this consent judgment shall be punishable by the

contempt power of the United States District Court.

23. Upon the entry of this order, Michael T. Moore shall be excused as attorney for those defendants he now represents and is therefore excused and relieved from any further responsibilities, with such being done with the full knowledge, approval, and consent of those parties that he does represent. The said defendants represented by Michael T. Moore having been fully advised of their right to be heard in open court should they desire to challenge the withdrawal of said Michael T. Moore as their attorney.

A few paragraphs of this consent agreement deserve separate comment. As to Paragraph 3, you may note that it does not specify whether or not drapes should be provided around the latrines. I noted that, too. No one raised the question and I certainly didn't raise it for them.

Paragraph 20 concerning the liaison committee occasioned a little controversy later. Paragraph 21, a face-saving device insisted upon by the State, occasioned more than a little controversy later, and later I will discuss the controversy. Paragraph 22 made violations of the agreement punishable by the contempt power of the Court. Normally when an agreement recites such a contempt power that means the judge does not expect to see the matter again unless one of the parties comes back with evidence of a violation by the other party. In a reversion to my earlier blissful ignorance, I supposed I was almost through seeing the parties to this controversy. As you may have guessed, this was not the case.

Number 23 looked after a special interest of the ACLU attorney who had thus far been representing the Rainbows in the case. Once this agreement was signed, the American Civil Liberties Union apparently would have unionized all the civil liberties it intended to for the Rainbow Family. Possibly, Mike thought he had more important liberties to unionize elsewhere. Possibly, his withdrawal was motivated by the fact that he was not being paid for his appearances in the Rainbow litigation. Thus, where Kip was *amicus curiae*, Mike functioned as *amicus iridii*, or "friend of the Rainbows." While it may be difficult to find the end of a rainbow, perhaps after days away from his regular practice and hours of trying to sell the Rainbows what Mike honestly was attempting in their best interests, the end of the friendship was not so difficult to discover. After several hours of trying to achieve their consent to what he was trying to do for them, he could see the end rather plainly.

But the end of Mike's representation was not yet reached with the achieving of an agreement acceptable to the attorneys. In litigation, a consent order is not a consent order until the clients have consented to it. In the case of Bob's clients, this was only a small problem. In many cases, an assistant attorney general can sign for the state, but in the particular context of this lawsuit, Bob's client was technically not the State but Dr. Levine, a State health director. He was in Atlanta for a conference. It became necessary to electronically mail a duplicate original of the agreement to Atlanta. This worked for the unsigned agreement, but a signature on an agreement this sensitive should not be a facsimile, so Dr. Levine then had to send the signed copy back to Bob by plane in order for us to file it in time to do any good. Remember, this was Tuesday, June 30th when we hammered out the agreement. Since June hath only 30 days, July 4th was coming no later than Saturday. Add to this the by-then certain fact that over 5,000 Rainbows were in the woods and you know that the signing of the agreement was not to be delayed.

If signing by Bob's client was a small problem, the signing by Mike's was a huge one. Who signs for the Rainbows? Certainly, Mike could sign for his clients. That did not answer the lurking question of who his clients were. Many times in the legal papers associated with the lawsuit, we all referred to the Rainbows as an unincorporated association. That's the closest category the law has to what the Rainbows are. They're certainly not a corporation, a partnership or an individual. But calling them an unincorporated association did not get us very far. As Garrick testified at the hearing, the Rainbows themselves have spent a lot of time talking about what they are and they haven't yet decided. The Rainbows have apparent leaders but they deny any right to speak for each other. However, when they are encamped in their gathering, the council assembles every evening. This daily council, like the one that determines next year's gathering place, consists of all those encamped who decide they are members of the council. Somewhat like certain Indian tribes, the right to speak devolves upon each in turn depending upon who is then claiming it. Very few decisions actually get made that way, but very few decisions actually need to get made in a hippie encampment. This time, one needed to be made.

I directed that the proposed agreement be submitted to council and that all parties reassemble tomorrow, Bob with his signed copy, and Mike together with spokespersons for the Rainbows, with a copy signed by some designated individuals with their descriptive data as to place of birth and address so that we could find them again if contempt proceedings became necessary. Mike pointed out to me that it was too late to take the agreement to council that day. I then allowed one more day or until July 2 and ordered Melanie to close court.

Just before I directed her to close court, I had recited the terms of the consent to the assembled audience. Since hours had passed, you may have assumed that many of the Rainbows had gone back to camp and that we would have little audience. I so assumed, and I assumed as wrongly as you may have. The courtroom was still packed. When I announced that it was apparent that the gathering could proceed, the audience could hardly contain itself. Had I not had Marshals in the courtroom, the audience might not have contained itself. At last court closed and they contained no longer. Melanie had called out, "Oyez, oyez, this Honorable Court takes recess until 9:00 Thursday morning." The word "morning" had not quit echoing when one of the Rainbows, I believe it was the fellow I've called "Ralph," jumped to his feet in the front row and shouted, "Thank you, Judge Dave!"

20 ✦ *JUST (OR UNJUST?) FOR THE RECORD*

On July 2, we again opened court. Nearly as many Rainbows attended as had two days before. The State's attorney was there without a copy of the agreement signed by his plaintiff. The courier had not made it from Atlanta. I accepted the attorney's representations that his client had in fact signed and that he had received authority to sign in his client's stead with the signed copy to be added as soon as it arrived. This caused little problem.

Mike was there, performing what he hoped to be his last representation for the Rainbow Tribe. But as his first act, he asked if the attorneys could approach the bench. This is fairly unusual in a non-jury case. In jury cases, attorneys often ask to approach the bench when they have something that needs to be said to the judge but which the jury should not hear. Sometimes, of course, it's something the judge should not hear either, but we have to listen and juries don't. In a non-jury case, though, there is no pristine collective mind of twelve to be tainted and approaching the bench usually serves no purpose. It appeared to me that counsel must have something likely to set off some fireworks with the assembled tribe. I, therefore, told counsel they could approach the bench provided they were not coming to the bench in order to blow apart the settlement. Mike wasn't sure if he was or not. He represented to me, and I later represented on the record, that the council of the Rainbows had in fact unanimously agreed to the signing of the consent, but a faction led by my old friend, Principle, had such strong misgivings about Paragraph 21 that they had consented only because they wished to acquiesce to the majority's desire and not because they believed the settlement to be a just one. Therefore, Mr. Principle wanted to read a statement of misgivings into the record. Mike wanted to warn Bob what was afoot so that he could make any objections. I told him I would overrule them. We sent counsel back away from the bench and Mr. Principle made his stand. He read the following statement into the record:

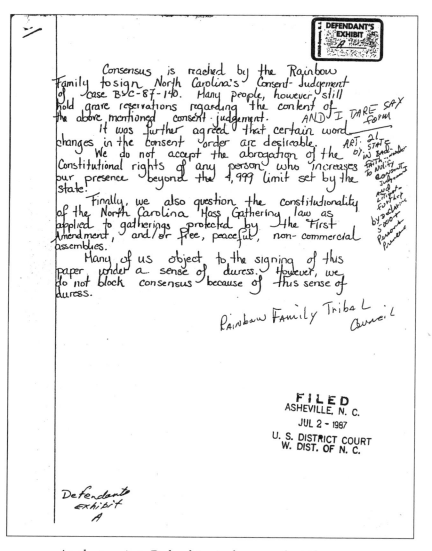

Consensus is reached by the Rainbow Family to sign North Carolina's Consent-Judgement of case B-C-87-140. Many people, however, still hold grave reservations regarding the content of the above mentioned consent-judgement. AND I DARE SAY

It was further agreed that certain word changes in the consent order are desirable.

We do not accept the abrogation of the Constitutional rights of any person who increases our presence beyond the 1,999 limit set by the state.

Finally, we also question the constitutionality of the North Carolina 'Mass Gathering' law as applied to gatherings protected by the First Amendment, and/or free, peaceful, non-commercial assemblies.

Many of us object to the signing of this paper, under a sense of duress. However, we do not block consensus because of this sense of duress.

                    Rainbow Family Tribal Council

FILED
ASHEVILLE, N. C.
JUL 2 - 1987
U. S. DISTRICT COURT
W. DIST. OF N. C.

Defendant's
Exhibit
A

At that point, Bob objected anew that the statement read into the record was not the one he had been shown before the conference. I overruled his objections since

I didn't think the statement or the objection made any difference anyway. As I said before, I try to follow the law on a given subject rather than my own notions as to what's right or wrong. However, this particular controversy had long since left the area in which there was any law to follow, and as Coot would have advised me, I simply tried to use the common sense God gave me.

Principle signed the consent agreement with his address and identifying data and so did Garrick. Counsel for both sides had already signed. I found as fact and concluded as law that the parties were bound by the consent judgment. I looked anew at Paragraph 21. As I had known all along, Principle's concerns were defensible. That paragraph did leave the State apparent room to litigate if more than 5,000 people were present in any 24-hour period. Though no one had stated it for the record, it was the consensus that by July 2, more than 5,000 people had been present for at least 24 hours. But the rest of the agreement seemed to take away from the State the power to do anything adverse to the Rainbows so long as they complied with the rest of the agreement. And so I addressed the Rainbows. I explained to them once again that I was not establishing North Carolina's law as being constitutional or unconstitutional. I was only declaring that given the facts of this case, my Court was not yet the proper forum to make that determination and no other court had jurisdiction at that moment in this case. I cited to them two cases (*State v. Smith* and *Radcliff v. Buncombe County*), the first of which said that North Carolina courts will sever unconstitutional portions of a statute to save the rest and the second of which is a federal appellate decision telling U.S. District Courts that we have to give the state courts a chance to do that.

I did not feel that the Rainbows were particularly impressed with the citation of authorities, but some of them did seem impressed by my black robe and deep voice, and the fact that I sat up higher in the courtroom than anyone else. I've always thought that these factors had a lot to do with a judge's authority. I knew one ol' North Carolina judge who said that every lawyer and every jurist needed two physical attributes to succeed: gray hair for a look of maturity and hemorrhoids for a look of concern. I'd had a little gray hair before the Rainbows ever came to North Carolina and I'm sure a lot more by the time I pronounced judgment. So far as the hemorrhoids, the case itself was providing enough pain in that region that I needed nothing else to give me a look of concern.

I went on to tell the assembled once again how I thought this settlement furthered the State's primary purpose in this litigation of protecting the watershed at Tapoco and the enforcement of health regulations insofar as possible at the encampment. I went on to tell the Rainbows that the settlement as well accomplished their primary purpose in holding their gathering. I commended the representatives of the Rainbows and their people and the State of North Carolina and their officials for what I described as, "the reasonable way which everybody had worked together to accomplish as much of the mutual goals as possible." I expressed my understanding with the "reservations of each side with regard to certain questions in the case." But I told them I didn't think the matters about which they had the reservations would create any problem as long as everybody remained in compliance with the order, and I told them that if anybody violated the order, then "it would have to be restored." I assured them that, "I'm exercising equity powers and I'm not going to use this settlement to impose anything inequitable on any parties to this lawsuit."

At that point, I could see in the faces of Principle and other Rainbows behind him the sense of relief, of satisfaction, of a belief that things were indeed going to be all right. And while I did not express it, I felt a strong sense of personal misgiving about what I had just done. I do not mean that I thought I had done the wrong thing. What I mean is that it bothered me that the result of this litigation and the future of the matters in litigation depended so near-totally on one man doing the right thing. It has long been a principle of American constitutionalism that ours is "a government of laws not of men." A principle danger of a result-oriented judiciary is that we then make the doing of justice depend not on laws but on persons. The law at its best must be the same in every person's case. When justice becomes a personal thing, it then becomes dependent upon the virtue of the individual judge. I know myself and a lot of other judges are not always perfectly virtuous.

I'd had this feeling before. I'd had it in spades. When I was a state judge, I used to hold domestic court about 40% of my time. About half of the hotly contested cases in that court involved the custody of children. When I held that court, I heard all the evidence, I found all the facts, I studied all the law, and then most of the time I simply had to decide what was "right" for the custody of that particular child. I always knew I had done what I thought was right, but I often knew that some other judge equally well-meaning and at least equally wise could reach a very different conclusion. We found no better way to deal with custody – one of the most important matters that can come before courts. But at least I knew in those cases that the law, in its benign neutrality, deliberately empowered me to exercise my own conscience. I have always believed that the principle reason state judges aspire to the federal judiciary is not the greater prestige, the life tenure, the divorce from politics, or the slightly higher pay, it's the fact that federal judges don't have to hear custody cases. I used to have what I called a custody case headache. It appeared whenever a custody case began, responded to no medication, and did not leave me until the case was over. I thought I had left that headache behind. Now, I felt it coming on again.

Matters of law – and particularly constitutional law – should not be left, I've always said, to the conscience of a single individual, no matter how well-meaning and no matter how apparently virtuous. However good a compass you may carry, however good a compass your neighbor may own, they're not going to point to the same letters if someone hasn't indicated N, E, S, and W in the right corners on the dial. However good my conscience, however good that of any other federal judge, we're not going to reach the same justice in every case if we erase the markings the law has put on the faces of our dials. And yet I cannot say that I would do anything different if I had the case to decide again. To act as I did – result-oriented, doing equity according to my own conscience, with questionable basis in law – is not consistent with my judicial philosophy. A judicial philosophy may sustain a court of appeals judge or a supreme court justice. A trial judge has to deal not just with the law, but with people. And when those people are about to be at war on a narrow bridge in the Nantahala National Forest, sometimes the judge must rise above his philosophy. Nonetheless, I remained troubled that several thousand people were satisfied with the result, were willing to sign a consent judgment, not because they thought the law was right or the system was working, but because of their personal faith in "Judge Dave."

I know Judge Dave and he ain't that perfect.

I asked the attorneys if there was any reason for another judicial visit to the camp. Each said there was not. I noted the relief on Beth's face, the disappointment on Melanie's. I ordered Court to be closed. This time a chorus of Rainbow voices sang out, "Thank you, Judge Dave." ☮

Part IV

Return to the Rainbows

21 ✤ THE RATIO AT THE BRIDGE

I had recessed court until Monday morning. That weekend, July 4th occurred on Saturday as scheduled. So did the official epicenter of the Rainbow reunion. At 12 noon on that date each year, the Rainbows gather in the main meadow, join hands and each in their own way observe a moment of prayer or meditation for world peace and healing. I did not attend. I did read the newspaper accounts and I watched the TV coverage on both local and national cable news programs. I did not cease to be amazed at how many different angles skilled TV camera people can use to photograph naked hippies without telecasting any naughty bits. I'm certain that the out-takes from their videotape are not only much more interesting than the telecast but much more popular with the production staff.

Monday morning I went back to the courthouse not expecting to hear any more from the Rainbows. However, having learned that ignorance brings bliss only so long as ignorance persists, I had taken certain precautions. I cleared my docket in advance so that I would be free to hear anything that might come up. I also brought a pair of jeans and hiking boots to my chambers. I noted that Melanie had done the same. While I might say I brought mine in the fear that I would have to return to the Nantahala Forest, I think hope sprang eternal in Melanie's very human breast. Nine o'clock arrived and we did not hear from the Rainbows. Nine-thirty arrived and so did Bob. He came puffing into my chambers. He gave me the good news first. "Judge," he said, "I've got Levine's signed copy of the consent. I filed it upstairs in the Clerk's Office."

This was good news. The record was now complete. I would have said that I thought my involvement was over, but I recognized that sheepish smile. There was now no other attorney in the case. At least no one was conspiring against me. Yes, they were. Bob was conspiring with his superiors. "Judge," he said, "I reported everything to the Attorney General."

"I hope he was well pleased," I said. I did hope he was well pleased. The Attorney General of North Carolina was an old friend of mine.* It's nice for your old friends to be pleased. I also thought Bob had done a good job of keeping the lid on a very dangerous situation and it would be nice for his superiors to be pleased with him.

"He is," Bob hesitated, "mostly." You've probably seen a pitcher throw a good curve ball sometime in your past. Such a pitch can seem to be heading for one spot outside the strike zone and suddenly break across the plate. I had the distinct feeling that Bob was throwing

---

* The Attorney General in question was the Honorable Lacy H. Thornburg. He is now United States District Judge for the Western District of North Carolina, and occupies my old chambers. I resist the temptation of hoping that he someday has to deal with a hippie gathering.

such a pitch. The "mostly" seemed to be the point at which it was about to sharply curve.

"He's not going to believe the Rainbows are in compliance until your Court holds that they are."

I summoned my law clerks and asked them if they were ready to go back to the camp of the Rainbows.

Beth had a great deal of other work to do for me which demanded her immediate attention. In other words, I don't think you could have driven her back with a buggy whip. Melanie, on the other hand, was up to date on all of her work and was willing to go if I really needed her. In other words, I don't think you could have anymore kept her from going back than you could have kept the swallows from returning to Capistrano, or the Deadheads from a Grateful Dead concert.

We changed clothes and shoes, mounted Bob's car, and rode off for the Nantahala National Forest.

On the drive out, Bob confirmed what Melanie and I had both heard from news accounts. On Saturday, the crowd had swelled according to various estimates to between 14,000 and 17,000. That's counting Bob.

"Looked to me like four or five thousand of them were fairly normal, next-door-neighbor-type Carolinians who had just come to see what they could see," he told us.

"Bet they saw a lot," Melanie said.

Bob nodded and smiled. "Did the rain bother them much?" I asked. The drought had broken that weekend.

"Nothing bothers them much. Just a lot more of them got naked and some of them rolled in the mud. I understand they think it has healing properties," he answered. "Like Melanie says, them that was watching saw an awful lot. Mostly the watchers didn't join hands in the circle, they just stood around and, well, watched. Of course, that's what I was doin' too."

"I thought you might go," I accused Melanie.

"I did not!" she told me, blushing.

Melanie is an honest person, and I believe her. If I did not know her to be a thoroughly honest person, I might not believe her. I know her to be a thoroughly honest person and I do believe her. I did not, however, press her as to why she was blushing.

A few miles back from the bridge, we again saw the lines of cars along both sides of the highway. The lines extended much farther from the bridge than they had on my last visit, but they were no longer continuous. They were broken by openings where you could tell that cars had once been but were no longer. They were breaking up more as we saw straggling lines of hippies, many carrying backpacks and blanket rolls, piling in and driving away.

At last we reached the bridge. Several very tired looking troopers were presiding over a large and varied crowd. Where a few days before we had seen purposeful lines of hippies going in toward the encampment, their faces happy and shining, we now saw the same kinds of people coming out. No longer did they move with vigor and purpose. Now, they shuffled, they ambled, they stopped to rest. Their eyes were no longer bright, their expressions no longer smiling. Some looked satisfied but weary; some simply looked weary. Some looked hung over; some looked spaced out. You may remember the Forest Service officer's previous estimate of the nudity ratio in the hippie camp. As I said, I thought her estimate was low. Whatever the accuracy of her estimate in the camp, the ratio at the bridge had always been zero. That is, there were no naked people in sight of the highway. When anyone did break North Carolina's indecent exposure statutes farther down than the alcohol camp, the troopers had been busting them. That was not quite the case on our return visit. The hippies coming out were mostly clothed. Only mostly. I saw several bare-breasted women shambling toward cars. I saw one dirty, hungover-looking woman wearing a leather thong and a ragged leaf struggling across the bridge on her way out. Apparently that fashion had become unisex.

So long as they were moving out, the troopers were mostly pretending not to notice. I'm convinced if any of them had stopped or started back in, arrests would have been imminent. But so long as a hippie was reducing the population by one, I'm sure that they would have had to commit a fairly serious felony to attract the troopers' serious attention.

We parked and greeted the troopers.

"How's it going?" I asked my neighbor, who looked like he might have been on duty since I left the week before.

"If I get home and my wife or one of my kids says 'welcome home,' I'm gonna hit them in the mouth," he told me. He turned away and shouted at the girl in the thong, "Hey you, get something on or get in a car!"

He turned back. "I wish they were all leaving, but you know they ain't." He shook his head.

"Still pretty peaceful up there?" Bob asked.

"Yeah. A lot of them are too wasted and worn out not to be peaceful, and the one's that aren't are mostly the ones that were peaceful to begin with. What bothers me though, you know we got warrants for some of them. One of them threw oil on Scott's camera and he swore out a warrant." Scott was the reporter who had sent the suggestion for the recruiting poster to the Highway Patrol back when the leaping Rainbow had been busted. "I don't know what's gonna happen when we have to make some arrests."

"I'd rather you and Bob discuss that without me," I told him. "Sufficient unto my Court is the trouble thereof."

"You just don't know, Judge," Bob told me. "Some of the arrests are going to be Forest Service misdemeanors for federal violations. I guess those go to your magistrate since they're misdemeanors but you know they can demand trial in your court."

"I still don't want to hear about it until I have to hear about it." I closed the subject.

Bob radioed ahead, stopping the shuttles and the trickle of live-in vehicular traffic now coming down the mountain. We started across the bridge and back up the road once again toward the camp of the Rainbows.

On the Rainbow side of the bridge, by the shuttle stop, we saw a sign erected in dutiful compliance with Paragraph 16 of the Consent Order. Large red block letters told us:

CAUTION — NORTH CAROLINA LAW REQUIRES
A PERMIT FOR A MASS GATHERING
OF MORE THAN 5,000 PEOPLE.
NO SUCH PERMIT HAS BEEN OBTAINED.

That sign complied with the Order. I liked it. Bob liked it. He did not particularly like the fact that next to the sign, the Rainbows had hung another one. That sign read, in imitation of the early Rainbow mailing:

PERMIT TO GATHER TOGETHER:
CONGRESS SHALL MAKE NO LAW RESPECTING
AN ESTABLISHMENT OF RELIGION, OR
PROHIBITING THE FREE EXERCISE THEREOF; OR
ABRIDGING THE FREEDOM OF SPEECH
OR OF THE PRESS;

OR THE RIGHT OF THE PEOPLE
PEACEABLY TO ASSEMBLE,
AND TO PETITION THE GOVERNMENT
FOR A REDRESS OF GRIEVANCES.

FIRST AMENDMENT,
UNITED STATES CONSTITUTION.

That sign was in black letters except for the words "the right of the people peaceably to assemble" which were a burning red. Nothing in the Consent Order said that the Paragraph 16 sign had to be the only one at the entrance.

22 ✴ IT AIN'T OVER WHEN IT'S OVER

As Bob drove us up the mountain, we met a straggling line of hippies coming out. Like the ones along the road, they lacked the purposeful strides and smiles we'd seen on the hippies going in a few days before. But, like the ones along the road, most looked well satisfied and mellow, if tired. We passed a few going back up. Presumably they'd been out for some or no purpose. It's possible, of course, that some were simply arriving late, but not many. Even the ones going up the hill looked like they might have been in the woods for some days. I had told Bob when I agreed to come that since there was no longer counsel for the other side, I wanted a few representatives of the Rainbow family to join us on our tour. He agreed that this was wise. I didn't much care whether he agreed or not since I was going to demand it, but it made it a lot more pleasant when he agreed. Fortunately, we found Welcome Woman again on duty at the gate. She looked a little tired, a little bedraggled, but almost as cheery as ever. "Welcome Home!" she told us enthusiastically.

"I didn't know if we'd find you here," I told her, "now that the gathering's officially over."

"Oh, it's not officially over 'til the 7th. Then we'll hold our last council and plan for next year," she bubbled enthusiastically. "There's still several thousand of us going to stay for several days. Even after the official end of the gathering, there'll be lots of Rainbows out here reclaiming the forest."

I changed the subject. I noted that she had taken off her Welcome Home T-shirt. However, unlike a lot of the other women I saw in the camp that day, she had put another one on. This T-shirt read, "NOBODY FOR PRESIDENT."

"Who for President?" I asked, looking at her shirt.

She smiled. "Nobody," she replied. "Who's going to go into the White House and keep all his promises?" she shouted.

"Nobody!" rang out a chorus of voices from some of the other Rainbows.

What politician is going to bring about world peace?" she shouted.

"Nobody!" came the response.

"Who makes better apple pie than your Momma?"

"Nobody!" Apparently, they had been through this litany before.

"So vote for nobody for President!" they all shouted together.

Daddy always told me don't make small talk. I got down to business.

"We're here for a compliance inspection," I told her.

She looked up at me expectantly. She blinked a couple of times. Obviously, she wasn't quite sure what a compliance inspection entailed. Unfortunately, I wasn't either. I decided to tell her anyway.

"We need to check to see that your people have done what the Consent Order said. We'll have to check the kitchens and fire areas and so forth for the right signs. The most important thing is we'll have to go toward the Tapoco watershed and make sure nobody's been camping too close to it."

Bob tried to help. "We need to look at the latrines, too, Judge, to make sure they're still all right."

I wasn't sure that was helpful. "I guess so," I agreed. Later that day we did and they were and that's about all I'm going to say about the latrines.

"Since Bob is with me, and he represents the other side, and since you all don't have a lawyer anymore, I'd like a few representatives of the Rainbows to go along on this tour." I did not tell her that we needed a few

representatives to go along, since none of us – Bob or
Melanie or I – was real sure we could find the way to the
Tapoco watershed. We did not have with us the topographical maps which were in the court file. The Rainbows' own maps were not to the same scale and did not
have a compass rose. It's also just possible that we were
a little uncomfortable about walking around unescorted
in the Rainbow camp. At least Bob and I were. Granted
we were wearing blue jeans this time. But there was
still a lot about our haircuts and general demeanor that
looked different than most of the Rainbows. I suspect
it had something to do with our expressions, which in
turn had something to do with our feeling uncomfortable in the first place. By way of contrast, before the
day was over, one of the male Rainbows had addressed
Melanie as sister and asked if this was her first gathering. I think she looked a lot more comfortable than we
did, and certainly happier to be there.

Welcome Woman brightened. She was already rather
bright but she became even brighter and said, "I'll be
glad to go with you. Come on over to the Main Meadow
and we'll find Badger or Principle or somebody with a
better sense of direction than I've got."

I had my own suspicions about why she wanted to
go to the Main Meadow before we started touring more
randomly through the camp. I suspected then and suspect now that she wanted more time for word to spread
among the campers that the counselors were coming.

That didn't bother me then and it doesn't bother me now. More on why a little later. For the moment, we headed for the Main Meadow.

When we came into that clearing we saw even more people than had been there on our last visit. A bigger percentage of them were naked and among those who were not the clothing was if anything more bizarre and varied than the first time. The fellow with the horned fur helmet was still wearing it but by now it was soaking wet and the fur was plastered down. He looked a lot like I think a yak would look if it took up residence in a pigpen. One camper was wearing a "sari" and a spot between the eyes like you see women from India wearing, but he was not a woman from India. One woman wore an army shirt, combat boots, and what looked like a World War II helmet liner. Nothing else mind you, just an army shirt, combat boots and a World War II helmet liner. And, of course, we saw all the work shirts, cutoffs, jeans, and general hippie gear, circa 1970, that we'd seen a few days before.

Welcome Woman led us to the CALM unit. No one appeared to be on duty. One potential patient apparently was laying in wait. She lay on her back on one of the outside rubbing tables, eyes closed, perfectly still except for a faint heaving of her chest that let us know she was breathing. Her mouth was sunken in. A set of false teeth lay next to her head. Her hair was gray, and not too clean. She was as gaunt as the Reggae music leader had been fat but she had at least one thing in common with him. Again, though she was stark naked, you had to look below the level of her flat withered chest to be sure of the sex. I guess it's reflective of my upbringing, but the idea of being naked at a mass gathering has always struck me a little strange. The idea of a woman the age of somebody's grandma lying there like that is somewhere beyond bizarre. I have a hard enough time imagining most of the grandmas I've known laying there naked, but I am sure that none of them would have done it without their teeth.

Since there was no one on duty at the CALM unit, and Welcome Woman apparently did not think the sleeping grandma was a likely source of information, we stepped over to the MASH table. The nurse with the T-shirt and cutoffs was on duty.

"Have you seen Principle or Garrick?" Welcome Woman asked her.

"I think I've seen everybody in the camp sometime today," she responded not particularly helpfully.

"You lookin' for Garrick?" a voice called out from the Information Center.

We looked around. The blonde Indian was back on duty. Well she may have been still on duty, but I presumed she had been off sometime during the days since our last visit. She did look a little tired, but not as tired as she would have if she'd been on duty all week. Besides which her golden hair was still nice and shiny.

So she must have been away to have washed it some time or another. Other than that she looked a little more entitled to carry the heritage of the red man since her once creamy bosom was now a bright rosy pink, but that's not the right shade of red.

"I saw him go up to Kiddie Meadow a few minutes ago," she told us, "and I haven't seen him come back."

While we were there I examined the posted notices at the Information Center and made certain they reflected everything about water, fire, and sanitation that the Consent Order had ordered. We thanked the blonde Indian and started toward the Kiddie Meadow.

The whole time I had been examining the signs, the blonde Indian had been talking. She wasn't saying anything in particular, but she kept talking. People who run information centers are like that.

"Wait a minute," she called as we started away. "Maybe that wasn't Garrick, I believe it was that other guy." All too often people who run information centers are like that too.

"We might as well go on up to Kiddie Meadow anyway," Welcome Woman suggested. "It's as good a place as any to look for him." I mentally added, "and a good way to kill a little more time while word spreads through the camp. She's probably presuming that the grapevine has pretty well spread the news through the Main Meadow area."

To go up to Kiddie Meadow, we had to cross the

whole length of the Main Meadow. I was not interested in going the long way through Barter Meadow again. When you've seen a three-ring circus once, you don't need to see another one for a while. By now though, the Main Meadow was pretty much a three-ring circus itself. Its once grassy surface was now a muddy red. Muddy hippies, some eclectically dressed and some not dressed at all, danced, sang, talked in little tight groups, or just sprawled about on the ground. Many more, most of them at least partially dressed, were streaming down through the meadow with backpacks and blanket rolls, apparently starting out to the real world. Near the center of the action the flow of outbound pilgrims split to pass a large circle of Rainbows who sat on the ground watching a naked man in a large floppy hat dance as he accompanied himself on pan pipes.

Just at the upper edge of the meadow where the trail from Kiddieville entered, we met Garrick and a handful of other campers, all in what I have incongruously described as traditional hippie attire.

"Judge Dave," Garrick greeted me. "We heard you were here."

I figured they had.

"We want to ask you about a few problems we're having with the government people, and some other things." Two or three others started talking at once. "The pigs are going along taking license numbers," one said.

"And they're taking pictures, and so was that reporter," another one put in.

"I told you not to say pigs," Garrick admonished the first, then he turned back to me. "Where is the liaison committee supposed to be meeting?"

I didn't answer. I didn't much want to under those circumstances and probably couldn't have gotten a word in edgewise if I had. Garrick's companions kept voicing complaints, and Bob had started arguing with them.

"There's nothing in the order or the law that says our people can't take down license numbers. You're out in a public place and anybody can take pictures here. Besides, I've seen some of your own people running around snapping cameras."

"Our people ask permission before they take anybody's picture. We recognize the right to privacy," one of them argued. Somehow I hadn't thought much of privacy in the camp since our first visit to the CALM – MASH units.

I held out my hands and tried to get everybody quieted down. In case you've ever wondered, it's a lot easier to restore order in a courtroom from a high bench with a U.S. Marshal in attendance than it is standing in the mud in a field full of hippies. Finally, I more or less succeeded – mostly less.

"Bob, you know, and the rest of you can learn, that I can't do anything about any of this or even say anything about any of this out of court. If you can make some more agreements, so much the better. If not, somebody is going to have to bring it back to court." I let Bob step off a little way with Garrick and his merry band to talk out their agreement for a few minutes before we went on inspecting. I had no idea that they would reach any agreements, but it made the hippies feel better, gave Bob a chance to vent a little bit, and allowed the grapevine to spread word of our presence, which was probably what Garrick had in mind in the first place.

While we were waiting, a naked woman wandered over and stood sort of between me and the little discussion group. She was about thirty or so, slim and athletic-looking with a lovely light all-over tan. From its uniform tone I guessed her to be a tanning booth user. She cocked her head and listened to the conferees for a minute and then turned to me. She raised her hand in the old 1960s "V" peace symbol and said, "Hi, I'm Susan."

I returned the peace symbol as I had done several times during my visits to the camp. Let me say that back in the '60s, I never returned peace signs. In those days we considered the peace sign a statement on the Viet Nam War. I never shared the prevailing hippie view on that conflict and as I said, I never returned peace signs. I will confess that at times I may have returned half a peace sign, but never the whole thing. But at the time of the 16th Annual Rainbow Reunion, the Viet

Nam War was long since behind us and I felt that the sign by now was only a friendly greeting and had no political statement connected with it, so rather than appear unfriendly, I had taken to returning the sign – the whole sign, not just half. I at least considered that gesture to be free of political content and I think most of the Rainbows did as well. In fact, I saw Viet Nam veterans among the State troopers returning the peace symbol as the love and peace crowd they were guarding offered it.

At any rate, I returned Susan's peace sign and expected her to go about her business, whatever business a naked woman has in a muddy mountain meadow on a pleasant July day.

Instead, she engaged me in casual conversation. This had not happened before. Let me clarify that. Many people have engaged me in casual conversation before, even many Rainbows have. What I mean is never before had a naked woman whom I had just met engaged me in a casual conversation at a public gathering. To tell the truth it had never happened to me outside a public gathering. Not even during two visits to the Rainbow camp.

The Rainbows seem to pride themselves on being very blasé about nudity. Indeed, it seems to be their unspoken premise that people without clothes are exactly like people with clothes. But thinking back on it, until that moment, clothed hippies had talked with my straight companions and me very casually. Even topless hippies had engaged us quite naturally. But naked hippies said "Hi" or "Welcome Home" or flashed us a peace sign and went on their way. Sometimes they talked with our Rainbow guides, but they did not stop and casually speak with us. Topless Rainbows did. Naked Rainbows didn't. Some of the naked males, particularly the younger ones, seemed to delight in greeting Beth and Melanie on our first visit, but even they smiled – or leered – and went on. They didn't stay around to pass the time of day. Some of the women actually made some, at least perfunctory, effort to cover up when we straights came along (like the young girl in underpants tried to get the woman with the extra-hairy pubes to do at the Barter Meadow).

The Rainbows project an image of being perfectly comfortable – or, more accurately, nonchalant – about total nudity. Perhaps in the case of toplessness they succeed. I guess in our society at large toplessness just isn't what it once was. After the 1970s heyday of topless bars and topless entertainment, there doesn't even seem to be a market for it anymore. I think everyone by now more or less realizes that when you've seen two of them, you've seen them all. Bra-less summertime tourists and unstructured bathing suit tops make toplessness itself not so different from familiar attire. You see young mothers nursing in shopping centers and on buses now. It's probably not that hard for Rainbows to be casual about bare breasts. With bottomlessness, they still don't quite succeed. Even hard-core old hippies, it seems, are not yet able to casually and naturally walk over to a clothed stranger in a public place and begin talking to him as easily as they would if they had clothes on. Most of them aren't anyway. This woman was the exception.

She stepped over beside me. Now when I say she stepped over beside me, I should emphasize again how thoroughly casual she was in her nudity. Not only did she show no hint of embarrassment or self-consciousness, neither her posture nor her movement indicated any intent to be seductive or erotic. Let me follow that thought for a moment much the way a beagle follows a rabbit trail – that is, meandering and wandering about without really knowing where the trail is going to end. There are two ways in which a woman can step closer to a man and speak to him. (There are probably two ways in which a man can step closer to a woman and speak to her as well but since that's not the situation we are talking about, I'll keep on telling you about a woman stepping closer to a man.) She can kind of slide over next to him, lean a little closer to him and speak a little breathlessly. She does this when she is trying to get something going between them. On the other hand, she can just step over closer to him as she would toward another woman and speak to him conversationally. She does this when all she has in mind is getting a conversation going between them. This particular woman stepped over and spoke to me as casually and unerotically as if she had been a fully dressed teacher and I was a parent she was greeting at a PTA picnic.

"Is there some kind of other legal problem about the gathering?" she asked, gesturing toward Bob and Garrick's little discussion group.

I had just been greeted and asked a question by an attractive naked woman in the middle of a rather public place. Being a mature, controlled adult male, I calmly and without any embarrassment responded, "Hi, (gulp) I'm Dave."

"Is there some sort of other legal problem about the gathering?" she asked me again as calmly and unerotically as if she were a fully dressed teacher at a PTA picnic and I was a dimwit.

Alan Funt from TV's *Candid Camera* once made a movie called, *What Do You Say to a Naked Lady?* That movie had showed among other things how flustered, embarrassed and tongue-tied people become when they are unexpectedly greeted by a naked person of the opposite sex. I was a 44-year-old, well-educated, professional man. I may not be a man of the world by some people's terms, but I've been around a bit. I was determined to respond as calmly and coolly as if she'd been wearing blue jeans and an opaque loose sweatshirt. Let's see, she just asked me, "Is there some sort of other legal problem with the gathering?" I, of course, should give her a bright, informative, responsive answer. "Uh, yes," I ad-libbed. Maybe not bright and informative, but at least it was responsive.

Melanie had stepped around to the other side to where Susan couldn't see her. Her eyes were dancing. She wasn't exactly smiling, but the corners of her mouth were beginning to twitch.

"What's it all about?" Susan asked. "I thought that was all worked out."

"Well, uh, yes — it was, uh, yes — uh, they're talking about — its mostly worked out, but — uh, some, uh, things — something came up ..."

Melanie's teeth were beginning to appear from between her lips. I think she was trying not to laugh, but she was beginning to make little fizzing sounds.

"They're not talking about bringing a bunch of troops in and arresting us all, or something, are they?" Her eyes got bigger and a look of concern crossed her face. I was looking at her face.

"No, no, no that's not — no they're not — they're not talking about that." I was not necessarily looking at her face. I did feel like I was doing a little better with the conversation though. Melanie pretended to have a coughing fit.

About that time a Rainbow walked up to us carrying a video camera. Though dressed in '60s vintage jeans and a tie-dyed T-shirt, his hair was stylishly razor cut and the camera looked expensive. I don't mean it looked expensive to someone on a government salary, this Rainbow had an expensive rig.

He didn't just start filming. Obedient to Garrick's claim of Rainbow custom, he asked, "Judge Dave, can I get some footage of you?"

This question was grist on which my mental mill could grind much more practically than, "What do you say to a naked lady?" Part of the dispute now raised between Garrick's Rainbows and Bob's officials was whether or not a person in a public place has a right to refuse to have their picture taken. If I told this camera-man "no," I would be at least implicitly deciding that question in the Rainbows' favor. If, on the other hand, I said "yes," that implied no answer to the issue. If there was no right to refuse, I could say "yes." If there was a right to refuse, I could still say "yes." Therefore, rather than foreclose the issue, I said "yes."

It only took me a second to run that question through my mind. During that same second, Susan had been running through her mind what the fellow had said to me. As he began running the camera, she smiled and said, "Oh, you're Judge Dave. I'm so grateful that you let us have the gathering." She reached out toward me. "I want to shake your hand."

The Rainbow kept running his camera. I was still awaiting confirmation of my appointment to the U.S. Circuit Court of Appeals. What if this guy worked for Senator Kennedy? What if Senator Leahy calls another hearing on my nomination and produces film of the nominee shaking hands with a naked woman in the middle of a national forest? I'm certainly glad she wasn't any more grateful than a handshake.

"Be talking to somebody about something," the video nut shouted to me. "I'm going to cut the sound on."

I looked down at Susan's face. Then I looked further down at Susan. Then I looked back at the camera. What do you say to a naked lady when the video camera is running? There was always Melanie. "Mel, do you think they're about through with their discussion?" What the heck, it was better than, "Testing one, two, three."

Melanie had another coughing fit. It was much worse this time. She was bending over and holding her waist with one hand while she grabbed my arm with the other one. Then I realized I was still shaking hands with Susan. What if Senator Leahy turns up with videotape of the nominee holding hands with a naked woman while being assaulted by a consumptive?

The conference broke up. Bob, Garrick, Welcome Woman, and a couple of Garrick's followers came over to where we were. I think some of the silly hams actually wanted to get on camera. "We can't reach any agreements," Bob announced, shaking his head and stealing sidelong glances at Susan.

"We'll just have to come back to court," Garrick announced determinedly.

"How will we do that?" Susan asked. "I thought our

lawyer quit."

Sometime between Melanie's fit and Susan's question, I had dropped Susan's hand and turned to face Garrick so that Susan was at my side once again. I glanced at her when she spoke. It's just possible I had glanced at her a time or two before she spoke. I don't know, I've never seen the videotape.

"We could do it ourselves," Garrick told her. "Principle and I have done *pro se* litigation before."

"What's *pro se* litigation?" Susan asked, looking back and forth between Garrick, Bob and me.

"That means 'do it yourself,'" Bob told her. "Kind of like when I work on my house on the weekend."

Bob's remark wasn't very funny, but it gave Melanie an excuse to finally explode with laughter. In a couple of minutes tears were running down her cheeks.

During the interruption in the conversation the guy I've been calling Ralph showed up. You never saw Ralph coming. He always seemed to slip cat-like out of a crowd or bush or somewhere you hadn't been looking. The big bone-handled knife was always on his side, always close to his hand. By the way, sometime while I was writing this I remembered his real name. It's not Ralph, but I've been calling him Ralph so long that his real name doesn't sound natural, so I'll keep on calling him Ralph.

Ralph hadn't heard what had gone before. He started things all over again. "I think these Feds and State guys are fixin' to cause us trouble, Judge Dave. Bob, can't you cool your troops off? You know when you've identified real baddies my security crowd has brought 'em out for you. Don't start hasslin' us over the small stuff." He looked at Bob, then back at me.

I should explain, I guess, that Ralph was entirely correct about the "real baddies." I knew from conversations with Bob, Mike, and Kip that law enforcement officers had identified a few wanted felons hiding out among the hippies. Somebody would slip a few quiet words to Ralph. He and a few of his friends would quietly and peacefully separate the fugitive from the crowd, much like a good sheepdog can take one ewe away from the herd. Before long they would produce him quietly and without a struggle to the arresting authorities somewhere down around the bridge so that no riot broke out in the camp. I understand they produced one of them unconscious, but no one ever told me that officially and no one ever asked me to take any action. A little more on that subject later, but for now, back to the Meadow.

I went through explaining to Ralph that I couldn't hear anything about the case outside the court. This also involved answering a few questions for him and Susan. The guy with the video camera kept filming all the time. In addition to everything else, Senator Leahy might now produce ten more minutes of film of the nominee talking to a half-dozen or so hippies while he stole sidelong glances at the naked lady beside him.

About this time Melanie quietly reminded us that what we had come there for in the first place was to find someone with a good sense of direction to take us on the inspection tour. Ralph was now here. He had a renowned sense of direction. I'm satisfied that he could have found anything in the forest even if he had never been there before.

We explained to Ralph what we wanted and he, Garrick, and Welcome Woman led us off to find the no-hippies zone between the Rainbow camp and the Tapoco watershed.

Our now-experienced guides started down through the meadow to the park service road ahead of us. Bob, Melanie, and I were a few paces back. She whispered to Bob and me, "I thought for a while there the Judge was going to ask Susan to take the tour with us."

Neither she nor Bob faked a coughing fit. Both of them laughed out loud. I know some federal judges would have been so pompous that they would have reacted angrily to this. I'm not that way. I simply chuckled and made a mental note to fire Melanie.

23 ✤ ON THE TRAIL AGAIN

Ralph produced a Forest Service topographical map and the hand-drawn hippie version and oriented them together. Though not to the same scale, he showed us where the features of the hippie detail lay on the official chart. To check out the protected area we needed to go back down the long trail past Mother Earth's, Hippie Hollow and the swimming hole. The swimming hole, as you may recall, was at the bottom of that hill. When you started back up the other side, you were climbing the ridge where the order declared no camping was to be. We started down the trail.

There were not as many people on the trail as there had been when last we were there. There were not as many campsites along the way, and apparently the campers who still were in camp had mostly gathered together at the gathering place. We saw a few Rainbows cleaning up their campsites or coming up the trail carrying their belongings. We saw some people who still looked like they planned to stay a while, but certainly the population was decreasing. The path itself, though, was a bit wider, a bit deeper, a bit muddier than it had been the week before.

I don't know if Garrick guessed that the path was on my mind, but he commented, "Very soon there will be work crews reclaiming this path. They'll rake up leaves and spread them on it and water-bar it with limbs and such. We've had volunteers raking leaves back on it every day. It's not as bad as it looks. Our volunteers just couldn't get anything done over the weekend, what with the big gathering Saturday and the rain. Anyway, you know there was a trail here before we got here."

We just kept walking.

We passed Mother Earth's, inspected it, and made sure all the signs were in place. Mother was there, but she had fewer helpers than the last time we'd been there. They all seemed happy and healthy, though, and were baking up a new batch of bread. "The crowd's going to get smaller but they'll still have to eat," she chirped.

We went on down to Hippie Hollow. They were in compliance too. I took a deep breath and made Bob and Melanie come with the rest of us back to the latrine. All the right signs were there, everything seemed to be covered with dirt and ashes, and nobody, thank heavens, was using it.

We walked on down the hill. We were getting closer and closer to the swimming hole and the sunning meadow.

Despite all we had seen on this and the other visit, I still wasn't real sure how I liked the idea of going past a whole meadow full of naked people with that young single female law clerk. At least it wasn't Beth.

But as we got closer I did not hear the shouts of laughter, like before.

"Aren't we getting close to the swimming hole?" I asked. I'd really been asking Ralph, but Garrick answered.

"I doubt if anybody's using it today. It's not nearly as popular since the weather cooled off. People that had been in it tell me that it wasn't ever warm, but since that rain it's just too cold to be much fun."

That made sense. "Of course," I nodded. "You know I've been trout fishing in these mountain streams during spring rains when the water would get so cold my feet would be too numb to feel the rocks through my boot soles."

"If it's that cold and uncomfortable, why did you fish in the rain?" Welcome Woman asked me.

"I had to," I told her. "I couldn't get it to quit raining."

"Anyway, even if the weather hadn't changed, I don't think that there'd be anybody down here at the pool," Garrick went on. "For a day or two after the world peace and healing circle at all our gatherings, everybody seems to want to get together in the main gathering area and mellow out. And then of course, other people are packing up and getting ready to leave. The swimming hole probably won't be popular again until it's down to the small clean-up crew. They'll need refreshing in the next few weeks, especially if it gets hot again. I doubt if there is anybody down there."

Just before we came to the first line of hardwoods at the near side of the meadow two young Rainbow women came through them toward us, starting up the hill. They may have been starting out to leave the camp, since they were wearing backpacks. If they were I hoped they stopped and got something out of the backpacks before they reached the road since the only other things they had on were tennis shoes. I don't think they were leaving though. They didn't have the totally worn out look – with or without a tinge of mellow – that the lemming flock usually seemed to wear. They were as happy and smiling as most of the people I'd seen the week before. I turned and watched them walk up the hill. Melanie turned and whispered to me, "Are you looking at their feet?" I turned and looked at her as soon as the two were out of sight around the bend. "No, Melanie," I told her, "I was not looking at their feet."

"They had on some of the most expensive athletic shoes money can buy," she whispered. "These Rainbows never cease to amaze me."

We went on into the meadow. Garrick had been correct. There were no people there, and only a little camping gear. Ralph got a topo map out in front of us.

He showed us how the actual features on the ground matched up with the lines on the paper. After the swimming hole, the stream wandered off to our right. Eventually, several miles away, it would join the river that ran by the road. Obviously it could not climb the hill, cross the ridge and reach the Tapoco watershed.

To reach the ridge in question we needed to turn aside from the stream and climb a hill we really couldn't see from there. I realize that doesn't make much sense, but it's true. The forest was thick enough on that side of the meadow that we couldn't see far enough to see what kind of rise there was in the ground. We could tell from the closeness of the lines on the topo map that it was very steep indeed. The hill back up toward the Main Meadow had been a steep walk on a hot day the week before. The hill we were about to climb was steeper, and we wouldn't have the benefit of the open trail. Ralph searched around and found us what looked like a small animal path. We started into the forest.

Since it had rained, the little trail, even under the forest canopy, was damp and fairly soft. It wasn't worn bare like the trail we had just come down, but was lightly covered with leaves and a little moss. As we started in, we could see signs that a few people might have walked there since the weekend rain, but not very many. I do not know what sort of animals had originally made the trail, but they weren't very tall. Deer are the tallest animals we have in those forests, except elephants, and I don't think the elephant had been there long enough to make a trail. Deer aren't very tall. We kept coming to branches low enough that even Welcome Woman had to duck and she's close to a foot shorter than Ralph. I'm taller than Ralph is. It was slow going.

We struggled about twenty minutes up a steep, winding, frequently obstructed path. Ralph had naturally taken the lead. I'm not the woodsman he is, or even the woodsman I once was. But I'm more of a woodsman than anyone else who was along. I was right behind him. The others were really struggling.

He stole a glance back and saw that they were lagging well behind. "I'm not surprised you're a trout fisherman," he said softly, "you're that kind."

"Thanks," I said. I took it as a compliment and an honest one. Though the use of language is my profession, if you don't understand what he meant and what I mean, I can't explain it. I knew what he meant.

"I knew you'd let the gathering go on," he said even more softly. "I can tell you've got a lot of earth energy."

"Thanks," I said again. If you don't know what he meant by that, I admit that I don't either.

He and I stopped together at a point where several thick pine boughs went across the path from each side. We crawled under and looked at the small trail ahead of us.

"Ralph," I told him, "there's no way anybody has been up this hill in the last several weeks. Let alone during this gathering. Let's go back."

He didn't argue.

We turned and rejoined the others who stopped struggling toward us as soon as they saw us coming toward them. I explained to Bob the reason I was satisfied and asked him if he was interested in going any farther. To the surprise of no one he didn't argue.

24 ❧ STAND FOR THE BENEDICTION

It had been a fairly cool morning after a fairly cool weekend. By the time we started back up the main trail, it wasn't morning any more. It wasn't cool anymore either. The day was warming up. After the struggle of the steep path, all of us were a bit tired. Ralph was in good shape, and he was doing fairly well. I'd spent a lot of years roaming those hills and I wasn't doing too badly. Melanie and Welcome Woman may not have had the energy they started with, but they were keeping on. Bob, as I have noted before, is not what you'd call slim. He is so short-legged, he was having to take at least three steps to two of mine. Every few minutes we would have to stop and wait for him. As we came to a straight, open stretch in the trail we saw that a pair of Rainbow volunteers were indeed at work on the path. A young couple with a bamboo rake were gathering armfuls of leaves and carrying them over to dump on the bare mud. Since it was a long stretch of the path and we were stopping every few minutes, we could see them uphill in front of us for quite a while. They were a slim, attractive young couple. His hair was dark and neatly trimmed. He was clean-cut and clean-shaven. She was sunny and freckle-faced with her hair tied up in a bright-patterned red bandanna. They looked for all the world like volunteers working on a public service project for the local Methodist Church, except that the bandanna was the only stitch either of them had on.

They smiled and waved as they saw us laboring up the hill, but went on working in silence. No one spoke until we had finally come even with them. She dropped an armload of leaves a couple of feet in front of me and then looked up at me and smiled.

"Jesus loves you," she told me.

I am a Christian. My great grandfather was a Baptist minister. My father was a Baptist deacon and Sunday School teacher. I grew up in Southern Baptist Sunday Schools. On a typical Sunday in my youth, we went to Sunday School at 9:30 and Church Services at 11:00. We went back to Baptist Training Union at 6:30 p.m. and evening worship at 7:30. Every Wednesday night we went to Church Supper and Prayer Meeting. We went to Revival Services every night of the week for one or more often two weeks every summer.

Now, I'm a Baptist deacon. I've taught an adult Sunday School Class for many, many years. As it happens my class has included preacher's wives and seminarians and others so well-versed in the Bible that I never dare go in on Sunday morning to teach them without several hours of Bible study during the week. But if you had asked me before that moment if anything in my experience had taught me how to respond when a sunny, freckle-faced young woman, naked except for a bandanna around her hair, looks up at me and smiles and says, "Jesus loves you," I would have said, "no." But something had. "He loves you too," I told her and we went on up the hill around the bend and about the business of our tour.

"He loves you too," I had told her. And I am satisfied that he does. I know that a lot of folks that taught me in Sunday School, and probably a lot that I've taught, don't think that greeting people naked with a "Jesus loves you" is the way Christians should carry on their witnessing. Really, I don't think so either. But when I think of some of the things he's loved me through, I am satisfied that Jesus loves her, and probably doesn't have to work at it as hard as he does loving some of the people who go on television and not only tell you that you are going to Hell, but seem very pleased about it.

We got back to the Forest Service road and back to Bob's car. We rested there a few minutes and refreshed ourselves out of a canteen he'd wisely brought. Then we walked on down toward the gypsy camp, detouring to inspect the Kiddie Village Kitchen, the Supply Kitchen, and a few random latrines. All the signs seemed to be in place. Everybody seemed to be in compliance with the order. The latrines, thank heaven, seemed to be unoccupied. Finally we came back to the symbolic shower curtain. This time the young woman using it was wearing a bikini and inspecting the water flow away from it was not quite as interesting as last time. Anyway, I found no violation of the order there. We decided not to walk all the way to the gypsy camp, but turned and started back toward the car.

25 ✦ MURPHY'S LAW & ORDER

When it seems that everything is going right, that's probably as good a sign as any that it's not. Hardly had we turned to walk back to Bob's car when a Forest Service jeep pulled up. The driver called to Bob to come talk to him a minute. Bob scurried away from us. He and the driver whispered excitedly to each other for a moment.

"What in the Hell are they whispering about?" I grumbled.

Welcome Woman giggled, "Telling each other where the naked women are."

She probably thought that's what they were doing. I probably thought that's what they were doing. That's not what they were doing.

Bob hustled back to us, puffing, a worried look on his face.

"Come on," he said. "Let's get moving."

He got us all hustled along the road, then caught me by the elbow. He pulled me a little away from the others and whispered to me. "A couple of your Forest Service's finest came in to bust the guy that threw the oil on Scott's camera. They didn't check with the troopers and they didn't know we were in here. Rainbows get upset when you make busts in their camp. We've got to get out of here quick."

I got Melanie aside and warned her. Our Rainbow guides are not stupid. Weird, maybe, but not stupid. They knew from all the whispering and pulling aside that something was up. They, Ralph in particular, began to glance around trying to figure out what was wrong.

By the time we got even with the side trail to the Main Meadow, they found out. A little crowd of irate Rainbows came running out on the trail. They were looking for Garrick and Welcome Woman. I know Rainbows claim not to have any leaders, but if a flying saucer landed and the little green men said, "Take me to your leader," I'm sure that a lot of the Rainbows would have led them to Garrick and Welcome Woman.

One of them shouted to Garrick. (One of the Rainbows, not the little green men). I think it was the one who called himself Conscientious Objector. "You ain't gonna believe this. Pigs came in and busted one of the Brothers."

This time Garrick didn't try to get him to stop saying "pig."

Some of them began shouting at Bob. Some of them were calling Bob a pig. Garrick was trying to get them to calm down. One of them started shouting that the trees were coming down.

That last remark may warrant a little explanation. Once before I mentioned that some of the Rainbows had felled trees across the Forest Service road. That had been to keep law enforcement vehicles out. Now some of them apparently meant to do it again.

Garrick and Welcome Woman were trying hard to calm their people down. Bob is a good lawyer, but he used to be a good cop. He kept moving himself so that he was between Melanie and me on the one hand and the ugliest part of the growing crowd on the other. He suggested that he, Garrick, and Welcome Woman go over to the Main Meadow and see if they could find out exactly what had happened. I could tell this was a ploy to get the crowd away from me and Melanie. I am sure that Garrick and Welcome Woman could tell that too. Whether or not they could, they readily went with him. I didn't know how many other excited Rainbows might come running down that road, so I pulled Melanie back into a little area between the road and the Main Meadow where a campsite had been and where the Forest Service normally maintained a little two-table picnic area. I could see the Main Meadow well enough to tell that Bob didn't seem to be getting very far. Finally he came back down to where we were. Garrick and Welcome Woman followed a little behind him trying to keep the crowd back.

"Come on," he told us. "We better just try to get out of here."

Some of the hotter-headed made it around Garrick and Welcome Woman and went between us and the road.

"Stay back," one of them shouted. "Those trees are coming down."

Ralph appeared in the small line of trees between us and the road where the excited Rainbow was shouting. I did not see him come from anywhere. So far as I could tell, he had not been there a second before, and then he was there. He just appeared. He turned to the shouting Rainbow. He did not touch his knife, but he held his right arm cocked, his hand near, though never touching, the carved bone handle.

"No they're not," he said. He did not shout. He did not raise his voice. But he was quite audible, and quite credible. "They may be coming down *sometime*. But they're not coming down while Judge Dave's in here."

The shouts stopped. The crowd parted. Bob and Melanie and I walked on to the car and drove on out of the camp.

26 ⚘ THE EYES & EARS OF THE FOREST

I mentioned a time or two that I really didn't care very much if the Rainbows got the word around the camp that we were there. While we're on our way down the mountain, I'll explain to you why I didn't care. I knew that they wanted the word around so that people would have a better chance to hide their dope. I didn't care if they hid it. This doesn't mean that I didn't care if they broke the law. It wasn't my job and it was no longer Bob's to conduct criminal investigations. This isn't just a cop out, as I'll explain a little later.

As soon as we started down the mountain, departing hippies started trying to bum rides. About halfway down, a man who looked like a weekend hippie looked up and smiled and threw up his hand with his thumb extended. He was at least my age, with a short, neatly-trimmed, graying beard. He was wearing comfortable-looking hiking shoes, khaki shorts, and a tie-dyed T-shirt. Longish, but neatly-trimmed graying hair showed under a floppy khaki hat decorated with various buttons and pins showing peace symbols, slogans and wise remarks. Bob stopped the car and he jogged toward us.

"You're picking one of them up?" Melanie asked.

"That one," Bob said.

"Bob doesn't pick up strangers," I reassured her.

The hiker opened a rear door and piled in next to

Melanie. Actually he was next to the gun box, but he was closer to Melanie than anyone else in the car.

He greeted Bob by name. "I'm through with my stint," he said, took off his hat, and brushed back his hair.

"I figured you were, Brother," Bob said. "Else it would kind of give you away when you piled in here with us." They both laughed. "Momma raised ugly children, but not fools."

There weren't many fools among the law enforcement working with Bob on the Rainbow assignment. I had assumed from the start that there were brothers like this one among the residents of the Rainbow camp. I'd been in and around law enforcement for a lot of my career. If I had still been advising law enforcement agents when the Rainbow gathering came along I would certainly have had some of my troops, after missing a few shaves if they weren't already bearded, spending a few nights in the woods. I knew that Bob and Kip and their troops had done what I would have done. It was not only logical; it had been evident to me from the start. Bob and Kip were simply too well-informed about the specifics of what was going on in that camp. They weren't just observing it as known straights on trips with the Judge. They had eyes and ears in that forest.

We'd already seen what happened when someone made an arrest on a relatively minor offense in the middle of the encamped multitude. As Ralph had said, and as I'd heard from Bob and Kip, the "real baddies" were already being surrendered up. That meant that what Bob's troops had to do was lay low in the camp, watch and listen. When they saw an offense that warranted action they could remember their probable cause and get a warrant and make the bust at a time when it could be done with the least danger to themselves and innocent bystanders. If something actually became life-threatening, they were there to take action. When they spotted a wanted felon, one of the "real baddies," they could feed the information back out and somebody else could go to Ralph to get the felon delivered.

Now Ralph's Momma had not raised any fools either. At least one weirdo, but so far as I know, no fools. He had to know that the information about what "real baddies" were in the camp didn't come to Bob and Kip by Divine Revelation. But so far as I know, and so far as I have been able to learn since, he never made any attempt to find out who were the eyes and ears of the forest. Perhaps he knew, but I don't think he cared. He knew they were out there somewhere, and he knew that so long as they were there, somebody besides him and his security committee would be seeing to it that the "real baddies," bikers and the hard dope people, didn't rape or kill or maim the gentle, bewildered flower children that he had decided to join and protect.

Our new passenger – Bob introduced him but, since for all I know he makes a habit of working undercover, I won't reveal his name – certainly was not a child of a woman who raised fools. He was really perfectly fitted out for his job. He hadn't tried to look like a hardcore, year-round hippie or dope dealer. I doubt that he could have done it. Some cops can, but they are few and far between. What he had tried to do and what he'd succeeded at was look like a sort of laid back, weekend hippie who worked a straight job somewhere and took a nostalgia trip when the Rainbows would gather. He looked like some guy so close to middle age that he had busted through its border, who'd been a hippie twenty years ago. For all I know, he had. As I've said, there were plenty of that type out there. He fit right in with them and I'm sure that no one paid him much attention. Of course, he was not alone. He had other brothers out there. I think I spotted one or two. I would not have spotted him.

"You got a ride when we get to the foot of the hill?" Bob asked him.

"Yes," he answered, "my wife's picking me up."

"Your what?" Bob almost shouted.

"My wife," the officer told him. "We pre-set a time days ago. I sent out a sort of a confirmation through some of the guys with my last message. She'll be there. She's taking me over to Robbinsville to make my report and then we're going on vacation. I've earned it."

"Earned a vacation?" Bob retorted. "You just had a vacation. You went camping."

We reached the bridge, crossed the highway, stopped,

and let the agent out.

He trotted over to a waiting car, and kissed the red-head behind the wheel. Some wise guy trooper shouted something about that being the third woman he had seen picking this brother up in the last two days. The last time we saw him they were headed toward Robbinsville.

We headed toward Asheville. ♥

Part V

Looking for the
End of the Rainbows

27 ✳ DON'T KILL ALL THE LAWYERS

As you may recall, while some unnamed hippie camera-man was memorializing on videotape my discomfiture and the all-over tan of Susan, Garrick and Principle were telling her how they could bring the litigation *pro se.* You might also recall that Bob explained to her that that's doing it yourself, without a lawyer. He compared it to working on his house on weekends. I don't know how well Bob does when he's working on his house, but I know that for the past six months I've been trying to fix two dripping faucets at my house. I keep telling my wife that I am as smart as any plumber. She doesn't challenge what I've said, at least not verbally. She simply points at the faucets which are still dripping. For some reason I am reminded of my dripping faucets when I recall how the Rainbows made good on their threat and came back to court without a lawyer.

Not that I found anything new in people trying to litigate without lawyers. Like any judge who's been on the trial bench for a while, I had seen my share of *pro se* litigation. Often *pro se* litigation comes from prisoners who have nothing better to do with their time. Since federal law provides that persons who sign an affidavit of *in forma pauperis* status, that is a sworn declara-tion of poverty, can litigate without paying the cost of court, the prisoner has nothing to lose. Therefore, we frequently see cases where some prisoner asserts that his constitutional rights have been violated because he has been subjected to cruel and unusual punishment, usually because his supper was cold one night. Or we get a *habeas corpus* petition (that's a pleading that says "turn me loose") because the prisoner did not get a fair trial. Sometimes this is because the prosecutor was prejudiced against him, his lawyer was incompetent because he couldn't successfully establish that thirty-nine eyewitnesses were blind drunk or lying, or the prosecutor and everybody else in the courtroom were in a conspiracy with the judge, evidenced by the fact that they all stood up every time he walked in.

One prisoner used to file writs demanding that I not only order the state prison to turn him loose, but that I make the government give him a ranch and staff it with a million or so beautiful women. His complaints were not very articulately drafted and I never could figure out why it was that I was supposed to do that. He filed so many that I stopped dismissing them one at a time and bundled up twenty or so for a mass dismissal.

Not all my pre-Rainbow *pro se* plaintiffs had been prisoners. One fellow who was free and working tried to sue President Reagan and everybody who had voted for him for some violation of his constitutional rights that he never identified. Since he had neither signed the pauper's oath nor paid the filing fee, I dismissed the case without making the Marshal serve it on all the defendants first. Unfortunately, he came back and paid the filing fee, and I had to dismiss it all over again. I still did not make the Marshals serve copies of the complaint on all the defendants. In general, as a lawyer friend of mine once said, "Getting into litigation without a lawyer is a lot like having surgery without a physician."

Thus was the case of the Rainbows. We left the Rainbow camp on Monday, July 6. On Tuesday, July 7, we received the first of several "*pro se* motions in the cause" filed by the Rainbows, asking me to hold the state of North Carolina in contempt of the prior consent order and enter various new orders requiring the state to do just about anything the Rainbows wanted them to. By way of example, the various pleadings, all of which included whereases, wherefores, and aforesaids, even where nothing had been said before, attacked the taking of photographs, videotape, or movies without the consent of the persons being photographed, videotaped, or movied. One demanded that the law enforcement officers be removed from the bridge, since it was in the view of the pleader a violation of the separation of church and state to have the representatives of the state at the "door of our church." Some complained about the authorities making arrests in the camp. None of these were signed by the person being arrested, and some did not even name the person arrested. That is, one or more Rainbows complained about the arrest of one or more other Rainbows, not themselves. Some complained indignantly that the Highway Patrol and Forest

Service officials were copying down license numbers from vehicles parked along the road and at the camp.

Now you may have noticed that none of the activities set forth in the motions I've mentioned thus far had a great deal to do with anything contained in the consent order that the Rainbows claimed the State was violating. Furthermore, you may have noticed that some of the motions refer to acts of the U.S. Forest Service, which wasn't even a party to the lawsuit or the consent order. The Rainbows apparently did not notice this. Bob, however, noticed it on behalf of the State of North Carolina and Dr. Levine. Kip, our old *amicus* from the U.S. Attorney's Office noticed it on behalf of the U.S. Forest Service. They suggested I should pay no attention to the motions whatsoever or simply dismiss them without a hearing.

I found these suggestions to be quite reasonable. Normally a judge reacts favorably to the reasonable suggestions of attorneys, particularly when the attorneys are suggesting something that the judge wants to do anyway. Otherwise put, I found the suggestions tempting and I'm normally not real good at resisting temptation.

However, in the Rainbow case, I made an exception. There were two compelling reasons for the exception. First, the Rainbows had filed one other motion which did pertain to matters within the scope of the consent judgment. According to that motion, the Forest Service was interfering with the ingress and egress of garbage collection vehicles taking recyclable wastes from the Rainbow camp to the nearest recycling center. As you might have guessed, the Forest Service wasn't doing much about the egress, it was the ingress that was causing the problem. The Rainbows could get out with their recyclables, but they couldn't get their trucks back in. The Forest Service was quite happy to bless the exit of any Rainbow from the camp with or without garbage, but as to re-entry, they took a very different attitude. Whether or not I blamed the Forest Service (and you can make your own guess on that subject), this was at least related to Paragraph 9 of the consent order.

The other reason that I decided to hold a hearing was that there were still apparently a couple of thousand Rainbows camping in the forest, and on Thursday morning, a couple of hundred of them were camping on the doorstep of my courtroom, expecting to have a hearing. Since it was highly unlikely that we would get much else done around the courthouse that day unless we had such a hearing, I exercised some more judicial discretion and held one more hearing on their complaints.

Kip objected to the Forest Service participating in the hearing. Well, I guess all of us except the Rainbows objected to participating, but Kip did so formally. He pointed out that the Forest Service was still not a party to the proceeding. I pointed out that even a non-party can be in contempt of an order. He said that the Forest Service wasn't in contempt. I told him that he might be right but I'd be able to tell that better after a hearing. I asked him if he really wanted me to have a hearing to decide that question at which the Forest Service wasn't represented. He grumbled a little more but we all went to court.

I let the several Rainbows who had filed the *pro se* motions get up and speak their piece. Then I disposed of the motions, one by one. As to the pictures, I reminded them that in our country with its First Amendment freedoms lots of people get photographed who don't particularly want to be photographed. You may have noticed that yourself. For example, when the television news people show us footage of some guy who's just been arrested for murder, he's nearly always ducking his head. When a news photographer snaps pictures at a New Year's Eve party, there are nearly always one or two couples who are trying not to look like couples when the flashbulb goes off. And certainly, when a Congressman gets caught with a stripper swimming in the Tidal Basin, he doesn't step forward wearing his usual campaign smile.

I told them that as far as the demand that the police be removed from the door of "their church" was concerned, I really couldn't do anything about that. They had two severe problems: first, it wasn't theirs, and second, it wasn't a church. The property in question belonged, not to the Rainbows, but to the people of the United States. If there was a church and state problem involved, it would arise if I deemed Forest Service land to be a church, not if the troopers of North Carolina enforced the law of North Carolina on the bridge where the Forest Service road met the highways of North Carolina.

As to the complaints about the Forest Service making arrests in the camp, there were several reasons to dismiss those. In the first place, they hadn't stated anything that was wrong with making arrests in the camp. In the consent order I had certainly not enjoined law enforcement officers from making arrests for violations of the law. I hadn't wanted to, and I couldn't have even if I had wanted. Of course I could have signed my name to a piece of paper that said that law enforcement couldn't make arrests in that location, and it would have been worth just a little bit less than the paper it was written on. Federal District Judges do have a lot of power, but our power is not unlimited. There are some things we can't get people to do. For example, I have never been able to get my kids to keep their bicycles out of the driveway. Also, we don't have the power to nullify the whole body of criminal law and the power of the executive branch of government to enforce that body of law.

In the second place, if there is something wrong with an arrest, the way you correct that is by defending the criminal case, not by bringing a contempt motion in some other action. In the third place, it wasn't any of the complainers' business in the first place. Before you can maintain an action in court, the law requires that you have something called "standing." That means that the thing that you are complaining about has to be some of your business. One person can't complain that another person's rights have been violated. Well, of course, they can complain, but they can't do it in a lawsuit. Again, that's an overstatement. You can sue about it, but your suit won't last long. Anybody can sue anybody about anything, but the lawsuit isn't any good unless the person bringing it has "standing." That is, you cannot legally maintain your lawsuit for the violation of rights unless you're the person whose rights have been violated. For example, a prisoner can sue for cruel and unusual punishment because his dinner was cold. He can't sue for cruel and unusual punishment because another prisoner's dinner was cold. If he tries to sue because of the other prisoner's dinner, the judge will dismiss his suit for lack of standing. If he sues because his own dinner was cold, the judge will dismiss the suit for some other reason, but not for lack of standing. In other words, the standing doctrine is a judicial way of saying, "Mind your own business." In short, if the lawsuit isn't about something that has to do with the person who brought the suit, then the judge will dismiss it for lack of standing. That's what I did with the motions that some people filed about other people being arrested.

As to the complaint that law enforcement officers were copying down publicly visible license numbers in a publicly visible place, I don't remember exactly what I told them, but frankly I didn't pay much attention to it. That brought us to the ingress and egress problem. As to that, I told them that I confronted all the jurisdictional difficulties I had had with the original complaint, and that the best way to solve it would be to go back in chambers with the lawyers. Since the Rainbows did not have a lawyer, I invited Garrick, Principle, and a third Rainbow, who will henceforth be known as "Complainer," to accompany us to chambers. I don't think I had ever before invited a *pro se* litigant into a chambers conference, and after that one, I never did again.

28 ⚜ WHO SHALL THE GUARDIANS GUARD?

As you might have guessed, a chambers conference that includes three Rainbows is not an altogether pleasant occurrence. One cause of the unpleasantness, and it's cause enough, is that the three Rainbows had been living in the woods for a period of weeks, subsisting, I suspect, on local and imported roots, herbs, and raw vegetables. There was some evidence that the raw vegetables included ramps. For those of you not familiar with the ramp, it's a particularly pungent wild onion indigenous to the mountain region of Western North

Carolina. To give you an idea of the potency of the ramp, when mountain schoolchildren desire a short unscheduled vacation, all they have to do is eat ramps. Not only will any teacher possessed of a sense of smell excuse ramp eaters from class, she will forcibly exclude them.

I recall once when I was in the eighth grade some friends and I ate some ramps during lunch period. Immediately after lunch our teacher excused us – forcibly. At that time, I lived about five miles from the school. My father worked the early shift at a nearby mill, and I use to ride home with him every day. I didn't ride home with him that day. He stopped to pick me up some three hours after I had eaten the ramps. I got into his car.

"You've been eating ramps," he said.

It was not a question, it was a statement.

"Yes, Sir," I replied, somewhat unnecessarily.

"Get out," he ordered.

I walked the five miles home and never ate raw ramps during the school day again. But while I had restricted my ramp intake, Complainer had not. Neither, I suspect, had he visited the communal shower – or any other shower. Further evidence suggested that he had been around several campfires, and some other strange-smelling smoke.

Now, I do not know whether or not you have ever been in a closed room with ramp-eating, herb-smoking, shower-dodging hippies who have been living in the woods for an extended period. In case you haven't, the odor is somewhere between that of a sweating mare trampling through a field of garlic, and a wet dog smoking a cheap cigar.

I looked around the room. In addition to the lawyers, hippies and judge, I had invited the U.S. Marshal for security reasons. I don't recall whether I had invited Melanie or not but she was there anyway. Up until that time, I might have suspected her of being too sympathetic with the Rainbows. Looking at her face and those of the lawyers and the Marshal, I saw little hint of sympathy at that time. I could tell that they all shared with me a burning desire to make this an extremely short conference. Unfortunately, the Rainbows did not.

As I was opening the window, Garrick made it all too plain that the conference might not be as short as some of us intended. Although I had called the conference for the sole purpose of discussing ingress and egress, Garrick immediately expanded it to include the whole subject of the guards at the bridge.

"Judge, what we all need to make plain to the troopers and other," he struggled for a word, "law officers," he continued finally, "is that they don't need to guard the people of Graham County from the Rainbows. We are peaceful. We're not going to hurt the local folks at all."

I looked at the Marshal. He looked at me, and I saw a little twinkle in his eye. The Marshal is from Graham County. He understood some things that Garrick did not understand. "Jesse," I said, "will you explain it to him?"

Garrick looked up at the Marshal quizzically, from which you might gather that Garrick was sitting down and the Marshal was standing up. This was not the case. Nobody was sitting down. I had not invited anyone to sit down. Sometimes conferences get over faster if people have to stand while they are conferring. Nonetheless, Garrick looked up at the Marshal. Our Marshal from the Western District was a man who nearly everybody looked up to.

Now let me note at this point that the U.S. Marshals are not career law enforcement personnel. The Deputy Marshals are, but the Marshals are political appointees. Therefore, some of them do not much fit the popular concept of U.S. Marshals. I knew one once who was a flower arranger by profession before his appointment. He looked a lot more like somebody's jolly grandpa than anybody's memory of Matt Dillon or Wyatt Earp. Our Marshal did not look like anybody's jolly grandfather. Not that he isn't a kindly man, for certainly he is. But he really looks as if he could have survived the gunfight at the OK Corral. Although he's thin enough to take a bath in a shotgun barrel, he's at least six and one-half feet tall, with a rugged "Lincolnesque" countenance, and the sinewy hands of a man who's eaten a lot of his bread in the sweat of his brow. When he talks, people listen.

The Marshal talked. Garrick listened.

"What you don't understand, Garrick," Jesse began, "is that we ain't so much protecting them from you as you from them. You don't know a whole heck of a lot about Graham County. You don't know that there's a bear hunting club up there that asked permission last week to hold their monthly meeting at the head of Slick Rock Road. You don't know how many guns and mean dogs those fellas take to their monthly meeting.

"You don't know that it ain't been many years ago that somebody hung a sign at the bottom of our County line sign that said, 'black man don't let the sun set on you here.' Only it didn't say, 'black man,' it said something else that's ugly that means the same thing. Now I know you have got a few black people in your camp, not many, but more than ever spent the night in Graham County before."

I'm going to interrupt the Marshal at this point, to defend Graham County a little bit, and defend a fellow North Carolinian whose name hasn't come up in this story. I'll start with that fellow first.

I'm talking about Andy Griffith. Deacon Andy, as you probably know, was the star, creator, and general proprietor of the long-running TV series about Mayberry, North Carolina. I once read something by a TV critic which criticized Andy's show because Mayberry had very, very few black people, unlike "all real southern towns." The critic was not displaying any prejudice on Griffith's part, but rather ignorance on his own.

What he didn't seem to realize is, Mayberry, North Carolina, is a real southern town. Only its real name is not Mayberry, it's Mount Airy, where Andy Griffith grew up. Mount Airy really has very, very few black people. This is not because anybody ever hung a sign on the city limits telling them to stay away, and it's not because anybody exercised any force or prejudice to keep them out. It's simply because they never were there in the first place, and never had any reason to come there in the second.

You see, Mayberry is a hill country southern town. Like most, if not all, hill country southern towns, the vast majority of the people who live there have always lived there. They are the children of the people who always lived there, and the grandchildren of people who had always lived there, and so on back to the early Scots-Irish settlers who were pushed there by the English to be a buffer between them and the Indians, and who liked it there anyway because its rugged, hilly-blending-to-mountainous terrain appealed to their aesthetics and recollection of home. They were joined in due course by Germans (Pennsylvania Dutch) who migrated down the Appalachians from the North, possibly in search of a warmer climate, or maybe just looking for a place with fewer Yankees in it. They haven't been joined by anybody much since, except around Asheville and other mid-range mountain towns where retired people and Florida folk know beautiful country when they see it.

The TV critic's mistaken idea came from the stereotypical South which represents only the lowlands. Those areas, indeed, have large black populations, just as Boston has large Italian and Irish populations, and California has a large Asian-American population. Those white and yellow Americans are concentrated around the areas where they or their forebears entered this country, and, of course, where they can find jobs and make a living. Black Americans are no different. As Jesse Jackson has reminded us, his ancestors did not come here on immigrant ships but on slave ships. The slaves of the seventeenth, eighteenth, and early nineteenth centuries were transported to places where there was an economic demand for their labor. These, of course, were the plantations of the South.

I might note that it should be obvious to all of us, when we talk about first families of America, that since the slave trade ended, thank God, a long time ago, many black families have been in this country a great deal longer than many, if not most, white families. Therefore, when a bigot has shouted at blacks, "Go back to Africa," the blacks would be at least justified in shouting back, "No, you go back to Europe, or wherever you came from, you newcomer!" Fortunately for the peace of the land, most of our black citizens have been too considerate to engage in such shouting, although, unfortunately, some of the bigots may not have gotten the message by any other means.

But back to why there are large black populations in the lowland sections and not the hill country and mountains of the South. As I said, the demand for slave labor was in the plantation South. Plantations, as *Gone With the Wind* and a lot of other stereotypical representations remind us, require large open expanses of arable land. Large open expanses of arable land do not exist in the hill country and mountains of Western North Carolina, North Georgia, East Tennessee, Western Virginia, or Eastern Kentucky. Neither do, or did, plantations. When freedom came at last in the 1860s, Black Americans often stayed where they were, just as White American immigrants before and after often stayed where they came in. In part, this was due to a familiarity with the area, and in part due to the economic necessity for work.

That's where the plantations were, and plantation work was the kind of work they knew. Some blacks went west, to become cowboys and cavalrymen. One of the great, generally uncorrected racial inequities of this century, by the way, is the Hollywood misrepresentation of the working cowboys and the brave cavalry as a lily-white lot, when historically the black presence was enormous. But be that as it may, they had to go a long way west to find that work. Just as there were no plantations in the upland South, neither were there ranches or cavalry.

In the decades since then, Black Americans, like other Americans, have become quite mobile, and move wherever there is opportunity and employment. Not many of the mobile Americans, black or white, have moved to the hills of North Carolina. There aren't many jobs there, and there aren't many other economic opportunities. There are exceptions to this proposition – Asheville is a conspicuous one. But even in Asheville, and the other towns where opportunity has existed, there have generally been a lot of local or near-local people ready to take those opportunities so that the influx has not been rapid, massive, or particularly diverse. Therefore, even in Asheville, where there is a noticeable black and diversified white segment of the population, there is still a fair chance that as a school teacher looks over her new class, she will see pupils whose parents were schoolmates of hers and, as she ages, children whose parents she taught.

But back a little closer to the point, which of course was not the original point at all: Mount Airy, alias Mayberry, is located in the hills of North Carolina, and the TV representation of the nearly all-white southern town is entirely correct.

Now, Mount Airy is a little ways back in the North Carolina hills on the edge of the mountains and has very few black citizens. Graham County is *way* back in the North Carolina mountains, and Graham County has no black citizens at all. The people in Graham not only do not have black neighbors, many of them may never have met a black person. For the most part, they are good people, and not unusually bigoted or mean-spirited. But this is only for the most part. Some of the mountain people have developed, in their isolation, a distrust of strangers, a distrust of difference, and a dislike of those whom they distrust. It was this unfortunate fact that contributed the Marshal's remarks to Garrick Beck.

Back to what the Marshal was telling Garrick. Jesse took a long drag on his short cigarette. By that time all of us who smoked at all were smoking. It may not have covered up the raw aroma I previously described, but at least it changed it some. He looked down at Garrick and continued.

"Anyhow, I congratulate you for finally bringing some black people into Graham County. You have a few of them sleeping in your camp, and that's probably more than ever slept in Graham County before. But some of those bear hunters don't like black people very much. And, what's more, they don't like hippies at all. And if they ever had liked hippies they wouldn't like them now. They've been trying to get permission to run their dogs loose on the Nantahala Forest. They have never got to run their dogs loose, let alone elephants, and they sure don't get to look at naked women when they are out there in the Nantahala National Forest, when the hippies aren't there. If you really care about your friends, and yourself, you don't want the law officers pulled off that bridge."

Garrick stood there quietly, apparently thinking about what the Marshal had said. He didn't express any agreement, but then he didn't express any disagreement either. Fortunately, he didn't express anything else, and we were able to get back to the subject I wanted to talk about.

In a short time, we were able to work out a pass system whereby vehicles, including the refuse haulers, could get in and out of the camp. The lawyers were quite agreeable, perhaps more agreeable than they would have been if none of the hippies had been eating ramps, and everything came together.

I went back out and announced that we had worked out a pass system, that I was dismissing all of the other complaints, and that everybody could go home. Melanie closed Court, and nobody said, "Thank you, Judge Dave."

29 ✢ MERRILY THEY ROLL THEIR OWN

What we had not said at the chambers conference or in court was how long the Rainbows got to stay. That is, the Rainbows who still wanted to stay. The paper was reporting, and Kip and Bob were confirming, that the Rainbows were trickling out. There were still people out there who purported to be cleaning up the forest, and there were others still out there. But there were fewer and fewer every day. By July 14, they were down under a thousand, and the Forest Service figured this thing had been going on long enough. The North Carolina Highway Patrol decided much the same thing, and left the bridge. The Forest Service took over, seeing to it that the pleasant idyll of the Rainbows would not be too pleasant and perhaps not too long, or at least not too much longer. There is a Forest Service gate on the Forest Service side of the bridge. In a laughably inadequate attempt to maintain crowd control, the Service had been locking it for several hours every night throughout the Rainbow gathering. On July 14, they began to lock it all day, every day. They let people in and out. Mostly, they let people out. If you were wanting to go in, you could walk around the gate, but you could not drive, unless the Forest Service unlocked the gate. Unless you had one of the passes, or otherwise convinced them to make an exception, they didn't. They didn't make many exceptions.

The Service also took some rather more direct action to bring about the end of the Rainbows. Once the encampment population got down under 1,500 or so, they began much more rigid enforcement of the laws of North Carolina and the regulations of the National Forests. Most specifically, on July 14, they began to enforce the fourteen-day regulation.

The fourteen-day regulation is a regulation that

makes it unlawful to camp in a National Forest for more than fourteen days. On July 14, the Forest Rangers served every campsite and every vehicle remaining in the forestlands with a notice to be out of there by July 29.

Needless to say, the Rainbow remnants did not like this very much. They protested to the newspapers and to anyone else who would listen (which by then was not anybody much) that they were just staying out there to repair and re-seed the forest, and that they would leave it better than when they came, if the Forest Service would just leave them alone. They claimed that they were bringing out tons of metal that had been there for decades. This is entirely possible. One newspaper reported that they had hauled out a mass of copper, covered with the imprint of vines and leaves, that the Rainbows could not even identify. The local people could. But then the Rainbows, or at least most of them, were much more accustomed to home-grown marijuana than homemade corn liquor.

A few of the Rainbows filed new pleadings in my court. Apparently most of the experienced *pro se* litigators were not around because they didn't file very many and the ones they did file weren't very good. I saw no reason to schedule emergency hearings, particularly since I would deny most of them as inadequate on their face. Besides, I had other things to do.

Granted, the Rainbows have their rights. But so

do other people. Specifically, the people of the Bryson City Division of the Western District of North Carolina have rights to speedy trials. I was scheduled to hold a bunch of those trials beginning on July 13, the day before the fourteen-day notices issued. I was engaged in doing just that when the fourteen-day notices went out, and I wasn't about to interrupt the trial schedule of other citizens to consider what by now amounted to very frivolous *pro se* motions from the Rainbows. I read their motions. So far as I can now recall, without exception, I denied them without hearing. They were all free to appeal to the Fourth Circuit Court of Appeals. None of them did.

As so often happens, during the second week of my trial term, a trial finished earlier than we had expected. In fact, a defendant changed to a guilty plea first thing in the morning, when we had expected his trial to continue at least for the entire day. I told the Assistant U.S. Attorney prosecuting the case, "Call your next case."

"Judge, I can't. Kip has the next case, and he's not even out here. We told the defense attorney and the witnesses that nobody needed to come 'til tomorrow, at the earliest, because we thought this case would not even be through today."

This was quite reasonable, and no judge could logically grumble about it. I grumbled about it illogically for a few minutes. Had we been in Asheville, where my principal chambers were, I could have gone back to my office and accomplished some work on continuing civil matters. Had the case the next day been a civil matter with lots of pleadings, I could have done some preparation. As it happened, the next case was a criminal assault on the Indian Reservation, and I had long since prepared everything I could. I was therefore stuck in Bryson City, North Carolina, with nothing to do.

Now when you have a case break down in the morning in Washington, DC, or New York, or Chicago, and you have nothing to do, what you mean is you have nothing that you have to do. There is plenty that you can do. In Bryson City, when you have nothing to do, you have nothing to do. Now a federal judge has a certain entourage with whom he can do nothing. I had a court reporter and a law clerk (Beth, not Melanie, I couldn't justify the expenditure of bringing two). They had nothing to do, but they were planning on doing it around the swimming pool at the motel. I don't like to do nothing around the swimming pool at the motel. Sunburn makes me uncomfortable, and besides some tourists from areas near the ocean might mistake me for a beached whale and begin lifesaving procedures.

I had a courtroom deputy clerk of court. He had brought his fishing pole. I had not brought mine. He had something to do. I didn't.

I had a probation officer, a fellow named Jimmy, who lived there in the Bryson City area. He had an active file of cases, and therefore plenty to do, but instead of doing it he thought of something I could do with him.

"Judge," he said, "why don't we go over to Nantahala and see what's happening in the Rainbow camp?"

At that point I had few options. I could go back to the motel and watch daytime television. But I'd already been in contact with enough stupidity. I could go over to the Indian Reservation and visit the gift shops, and perhaps pay $5.00 for a painted rock tied to a stick, or a headdress of seven turkey feathers sewn together in Taiwan. Or I could go over to Nantahala with Jimmy and see what was happening in the Rainbow camp.

As Jimmy and I were going over to Nantahala, I told him, "Don't expect very much now, but you've never seen anything like what was going on over there when the Rainbows were out in force."

"I've seen something like it," he said. "I was at Woodstock. I don't guess there was loud rock music at the Rainbow Festival, but otherwise it sounds like there was a lot of similarity. You know, a bunch of naked people running around, a lot of people smoking dope, everybody swapping this and that for the other, pretty much what I understand went on with the Rainbows."

I had to admit there were certain similarities. I knew that at the time of the Woodstock happening Jimmy couldn't have been more than nineteen or twenty, and I didn't ask him what role he played in that historic event. Somehow, I don't think he would have told me if I had asked.

At any rate, we made it to the bridge. There were no troopers stationed there.

We crossed the bridge. There were no signs posted there. There was a closed Forest Service gate, a chain, and a padlock. There were also two fairly large Forest Rangers. They asked who we were and why we wanted to go up that road. I admitted I was the judge, and told them, "I'd just like to see how bad a mess it's in."

I didn't know whether that part about me being the judge would impress them or not, since one way to look at it was I was the guy who had let this thing go on that had been so much trouble. On the other hand, they knew it had been a lot of trouble to me too. They laughed, opened the lock, and let us in.

As we started up the road, one of them shouted to us, "Judge, don't expect it to be much like it was when you were up there before. Most of them hippies, thank God, have gone home."

We passed no alcohol camp, no rickety, make-shift transit vehicles, and no throngs of happy people going in or mellow lemmings coming out. We did see a few stragglers coming down the mountain, carrying back-packs toward the gate.

When we got to the Welcome Center, it wasn't there anymore. Even Welcome Woman wasn't there anymore. The crowds were gone. We drove on down the dirt road to the gypsy camp, and it wasn't there anymore either. On the way we passed the Krishna camp. It wasn't there, and neither was the elephant. We could tell there were still people around, but they weren't doing very much. Granted, it was by then the hottest part of the day and there may have been reclamation going on in the mornings and evenings, but there wasn't much of anything going on in the hottest part of the day.

We drove back toward the place where the Welcome Center had been, parked Jimmy's truck, and walked over through what had once been the Main Meadow. We could see that the ground had been raked up, and dried grass strewn across the surface, presumably covering new seeds. I believed then, and later confirmed, that raking the surface of clay-type soil that has been packed down that hard does not give grass enough room to form roots, and the Forest Service later had to bring in heavy equipment, till the ground, and start over. There were a few tents and make-shift campsites around the shady edges of the Meadow. We saw a few people, most of them sleeping, or lolling on the ground talking. We didn't see any naked people. Jimmy was beginning to look a little disappointed.

We walked back across the dirt road, and down the path a little ways to look where Mother's, Hippie Hollow, and the other related facilities had been. They weren't there anymore. The Rainbows had water-barred the path with poles, and covered it with leaves, and we did see a few people working on the reclamation of that area.

We walked back through the woods toward the little stream. We could hear childish laughter along with the tinkling water. When we got there we did find two naked girls enjoying the creek, but their combined age could not have been much more than seven. A woman in a long peasant dress lay on the bank in a shady place near the creek. She had probably come there to watch the children, but she had stayed to sleep.

We walked back to the road, and back past an area where I had seen several campsites on my prior visits. As we looked down through the woods toward a small meadow, we spotted what I think Jimmy had been looking for. There was a naked young woman sitting down there on a log near a tent talking to a fully clothed man. However, as we crashed down the bank, we realized anew that the authorities had begun to enforce the indecent exposure laws, as she ran for the tent faster than Jimmy could crash through the woods.

All the view he got of her was much the same view a hapless hunter gets of a Smoky Mountain deer, that is a white tail disappearing from view.

We came to her companion, Jimmy coming somewhat sooner than I did. He spoke to the man sitting on the log.

"We didn't mean to scare away your friend," he told him. Jimmy was entirely sincere in this apology.

The stranger on the log took a cloth sack of something and a pack of rolling papers out of his shirt pocket.

As he rolled a smoke, he answered Jimmy, "You didn't scare nobody."

I got there just as the stranger lit his product. I sniffed the air. I smelled tobacco, so I felt free to join the conversation group. Before I spoke, I mentally assessed the man on the log. He wasn't quite meeting Jimmy's eyes when he spoke to him, and he didn't meet mine when I said hello. His eyes were a little blank, or vacant. He was at least my age, probably several years more. Not only his clothes, but his skin had a weathered, faded appearance that let you know the man wearing them had spent a lot of time in them and gone a lot of miles on hard road. As we had passed other makeshift campsites, I had suspected that the hobo contingent was still well-represented among the few hundred campers still on-site. I now knew it for sure.

"You all still kinda fixin' up the area?" I asked him. I wasn't particularly interested in his answer, but it gave me something to say. He pulled on his hand-rolled cigarette, and thought a minute before answering. Actually, I don't think he thought a minute but at least he sat there in silence for a minute before answering.

"Ya, I guess some folks are," he observed at last. He didn't say what he was doing. There was no polite way we could ask.

"You enjoying life?" Jimmy asked him.

There was another long pause. "Ya, I guess some folks are." That answer had served him well once, and he was sticking to it. Somewhere on the road he had learned not to give very much information to straight-looking strangers, and he intended to put that lesson to use.

About this time, the young woman who had fled at our approach came back out of the tent. I had stepped around the log, so that my back was toward her as she approached, but I could tell from the look of disappointment in Jimmy's face that she was by now fully dressed. She was also a bit more of a conversationalist than the man on the log.

"Hi," she said as she sat back down on the log. I realize this isn't the most stimulating conversation in the world, but then it is more than the hobo had volunteered.

She looked to be a good deal less than half the age of her companion. She wore faded, cut-off blue jeans, and a dirty T-shirt advertising a lounge in Atlanta, Georgia. Despite the fact that she was of a more recent vintage, she also appeared to be a high-mileage model. But the blank look on her rather pretty little face was probably not acquired in hobo jungles. In fact, I suspected from the look in her eyes that rough cut tobacco was not the only thing being smoked in this left-over campsite. But it was the only thing she was going to smoke in front of us right then. She took the butt from the man's stained, yellow fingers, inhaled the last drag, and put it out in the clay at her feet. "You all lookin' for anything in particular?" she asked us.

I was hesitant to answer her. Jim wasn't. Well, he

may have been hesitant, but he did answer her. "No, we're just lookin' around. The Judge, here, had been out a couple of times during the Reunion, and he wanted to see how it looked afterward." The young woman looked a bit impressed when he said "Judge." The man was more impressed by the pack of cigarettes Jim pulled out of his pocket.

"Can I bum one of them readyrolled?" he asked, almost looking Jimmy in the eye.

Jimmy handed him the pack. He got out one ciga-rette and handed the pack to the girl, who pulled one for herself. Then she began to talk again.

"Yeah, I heard down in Georgia that some Judge was lettin' them have this thing, you know. I thought, you know, I'd come up here, and kind of, you know, see what was, you know, happenin'." A real conversation starter.

"You're from Georgia?" Jimmy asked her.

"Yeah," she replied. "Well, I'm not from there, you know, but I've been staying there. I've been, you know, working at this club."

I wasn't about to ask her what sort of working she'd been doing. Jimmy was. "Are you a waitress?" he asked.

"I've been, you know, stripping, dancing, really, you know, exotic stuff, real artistic."

"You going back there now that the gathering is over?" Jimmy asked her.

"No, I can't," she replied. "I didn't tell them I wasn't coming in that last night. I just, you know, took off for here. So, I don't guess I have a job there. I don't know where I'm going. You know anywhere around here I could get work stripping?" She looked at Jim expectantly.

"No," I interrupted. I don't think Jim would have started haggling with her about a price, but I wasn't taking any chances. I bid them good day and pulled Jim on back up the bank toward the car.

We rode back down the mountain through the gate and on back towards Bryson City. We rode in silence for a while. I think each of us was a little miffed at the other. I think Jim was a little miffed at me and the hobo because we got to see the naked women running around the Rainbow camp and he didn't. I was a little miffed at him for a couple of reasons. In the first place, I thought it was immature of him to be jealous. I was also a little miffed because he got to go to Woodstock and I didn't.

However, Jim and I are a forgiving lot and we were soon speaking again. But while we were riding along, I began to think that what we had just seen in the Rainbow camp made a fair parallel to what society as a whole had seen of the hippie movement. In the '60s, the hippies entered society the way the Rainbows had entered the Nantahala Forest. They weren't going to abide by anybody else's rules, or learn from anybody else's experience. They were convinced they were going to do things their own way, and leave society better than they had found it. Instead, they left a lot of damage that other people would have to repair. They left behind the ill effects of the drug culture, and some young people who could not go back home and did not know where they were going instead.

Oh, yes, when the hippies entered society in the 1960s, sex was still a beautiful private thing between a man and a woman with a foundation in love. And that's the way it was in Graham County before the Rainbows arrived. Granted, neither society nor Graham County really lived up to the ideal, but at least vice paid hypocritical tribute to that virtue. Then the hippies fought the sexual revolution. Sex lost.

As I was musing, Jim was driving. We pulled into a roadside country store. "Need a soda?" I asked. I did.

"I guess so," said Jim. "But mostly I need some cigarettes. Those folks never gave back my readyrolled."

30 ✤ FREE THE RAINBOW EIGHT

As the next several days passed, campers continued to trickle out of the Rainbow remnant. You'd see them occasionally, hitchhiking or driving down the road in their beat-up vans and other vehicles. I finished holding court in Bryson City, and went back to Asheville for more routine judicial tasks while still awaiting confirmation. July 29 came, as expected. Not all the campers had left the Nantahala Forest, also as expected. On July

30, the Forest Rangers entered, and ordered immediate departure by those who were left. They arrested some who did not comply. I do not believe they arrested all who did not comply, but they arrested some. People who seemed to be making a good faith effort to get out were not arrested. They may have been hassled, but not arrested. Those who did not make such effort were arrested, or at least as many as the Service had time to arrest.

The Forest Service brought eight of the arrestees back to Asheville for hearings that day before our United States Magistrate. It would be his duty to decide such things as bond, sufficiency of arrest process, and trial date. This he would decide at hearings in his courtroom, which was directly upstairs from my chambers. Melanie went upstairs to take a look at what was happening. She brought back a report. I had not ordered her to bring back a report. I had not requested that she bring back a report. I am not even sure that I knew she was going. Nonetheless, she brought back a report. "Judge," she said, "I've been checking out the Rainbows."

"Why don't I find that surprising?" I asked her.

She ignored my comment. "It could get ugly."

"I've seen the Rainbows before. A lot of them are already ugly," I responded.

She went on undeterred. "These aren't our friends up there." I'd never considered the Rainbows particularly friends of mine.

"I don't mean just the eight that are in court. There's a bunch of other strange looking people milling around in the hall." If they had been at the Rainbow camp and hadn't been strange looking, that would have been strange looking. "One woman is carrying a sign that says 'Free the Rainbow Eight.'"

"Yeah, just keep me posted." I waved her out the door.

Later she came back, more excited than ever. "Judge, the Magistrate is through with about six of the defendants. They are not happy with what he has done. They're likely to be more unhappy when he gets through with the other two."

"Okay," I told her, "let them appeal to me."

"That's what I'm afraid of, Judge," she said. "I've been listening to them in the hall and they're going to come looking for you just as soon as the hearings are over. I've talked to one of the Deputy Marshals, and we think you should leave early so that they can't find you."

It was by then about four o'clock in the afternoon. I normally work until six o'clock or later. I normally am not in the habit of letting a law clerk and a Deputy Marshal decide when I quit early. This time I made an exception. Judges can exercise discretion. Discretion is the better part of valor. I exercised the better part of valor and left early.

The Deputy was waiting for me outside my chambers. He escorted me to my car. I wasn't particularly afraid of physical violence, but it was nice to have someone to carry my briefcase. Then I drove toward home. On the way to my house, just before the turn where I left the main highway, was a little place of business called the Neighborhood Grocery and Filling Station. Since my gas gauge was dropping toward empty, and the car didn't run very well on fumes, I pulled in and filled up. As it happened I had skipped lunch that day rather than go downstairs to a snack shop that I was aware was likely to be filled with Rainbows; I was about as empty as my gas tank. So I went inside to get a soft drink and a pack of crackers. I liked to get an occasional soft drink and a pack of crackers at the Neighborhood Grocery. As it happened, most of the people who hang around that store don't know who I am, and don't even suspect me of being a judge. I think it's a very comfortable place to be in. On the way in, I stopped and scratched Ole Red's head. Ole Red was a superannuated Irish Setter who liked to hang around outside the store because he liked people, and because people liked him and fed him little tidbits from time to time. That day Ole Red was lying on the full service island. When I had made by purchase, I looked back out the door. Bubba, one of the fellows who worked there, was pumping gas into a hippie van. The van looked like it might be, and it turns out it was, carrying some of the last campers away from the Rainbow festival. Bubba stepped around to clean the windshield. It took Bubba an exceptionally long time to clean the windshield.

Finally, Bubba came in carrying money to make change. He was unusually excited for a man just bringing in a handful of bills to make change.

"Boys," he whispered hoarsely, "You ain't going to believe it. There's a man and a woman and three young-uns in that van, and all any of 'em has got on between them and the Lord is that the man and woman are wearing little cutoff shorts."

I was sitting on an orange crate, drinking my soda. A storekeeper and two regular customers were standing in my immediate vicinity. All three of them suddenly decided that they needed to go feed something to Ole Red. Two of them nearly knocked me off the orange crate, and I had to grab my drink to keep it from being kicked over.

Bubba went over to the cash register and was hurriedly trying to sort out the proper change. He looked up and saw me. Surprise was evident in his face. "Ain't you goin' to feed Ole Red too?" he asked.

I chuckled. "Bubba, I'm forty-odd years old and a married man. I've seen a woman's chest before. If those boys want to make spectacles out of themselves craning their necks to look in that van while they pretend to feed that poor ole dog, that's their business."

Bubba slowed down a little. He mustered his dignity, walked slowly back to the van, and handed the driver the change without looking in the window.

Epilogue

I never saw the Rainbows again, at least not collectively. The Magistrate handled all the misdemeanants, except one or two who demanded a trial in my court. There were a few felons for my court out of the Rainbow Reunion. Therefore, I saw a few of the Rainbows, one at a time. I will confess that I thought about them from time to time, and at times thought about writing this book. What finally caused me to take the time to start it was, as I said in the prologue, a request from one of my law clerks – a request that came in the spring of the following year.

By then I had been confirmed for the Court of Appeals, and moved bag, baggage, and law clerks to Washington, DC. I read in the Washington paper, one morning in late May, that somewhere in a national forest in Northern Texas the Rainbows were beginning to gather for their annual reunion. Just after I put that paper down, Melanie came into my chambers.

"Judge," she asked me, "Can I have a few days off at the beginning of July? Just enough time to go to Texas for a few days and come back?"

It turned out that she was kidding – I think. ❀

Garrick Beck's
Reflections
on Judge Dave

In the true storyteller's tradition Judge Dave Sentelle weaves a tapestry made of many different yarns. The Judge's colorful account of the Rainbow Family Gathering in North Carolina's Nantahala National Forest over that July 4th weekend in 1987 leaves very few stones unturned along those woodland trails that he so comfortably, in his writings, lets us walk along beside him.

Still, he does leave out a few choice mentions and moments, and since I have the good fortune to have figured admirably in his accounting, I should like to take on the assignment of filling out his ledger with a few additional perspectives. Actually and honestly, there is precious little in the whole of his telling that I find inaccurate.

1 ✷ TO CRACK THE NUT, YOU ONLY HAVE TO CRACK THE NUTSHELL

Let me begin with a piece of the legal puzzle most notably missing: The Mass Gathering Act of North Carolina was one of many such laws hastily enacted in the aftermath of the famous Woodstock concert of the summer of 1969. I believe almost two-thirds of the states passed such acts in efforts that varied widely. Some were written to make certain that a rock and roll event of that sort or scale would never ever be able to occur within a particular state's boundaries. And other so-called "Woodstock Laws" were efforts to legislate that if such an event were to occur within a particular state that it should have to conform to certain standards of sanitation and safety, and that the promoters would provide the insurance and bonding necessary to protect the state and public from what damage might occur.

Most of these laws were full of legalistic problems that are so often the result of haste. The North Carolina law was one of these. Its fundamental problem, at least insofar as it related to the Rainbow People, was that it lumped together both commercial and non-commercial expressive events.

Quite clearly the state has the right in innumerable ways to regulate commerce ... but expressive, non-commercial assemblies, that's another matter. The history of our country is rich with the legacy of protecting the rights of people peaceably to assemble. And there are many protections that Supreme Court doctrine has upheld as priceless heritages that cannot simply be undone because a state legislature wills it so.

This was the case with North Carolina's Mass Gathering Act. It commanded of commercial events many reasonable requirements that someone wishing to make a profit from some kind of assembly could reasonably be required to ante up; but that some group wishing say, to hold a memorial prayer, or wishing to march in protest, or to hold a peaceful vigil in support of this that or the other could never lawfully – under the constraints of Supreme Court rulings on First Amendment law – be required to comply with. Such as: insurance and liability bonding; restriction of numbers; demands for particular services; indemnification of the state; and so on.

And even worse. In their haste to enact, the State Legislature left out a severability clause. So, if a certain section of the law was to be found improper or uncon-stitutional, it could not be separated and removed from the rest of the law. No, the whole of the Mass Gathering Act would fail and fall. And yet, this was the very act that the state was using for very good purpose to regu-late outdoor stock car races, amusement carnivals, and bluegrass concerts.

If the state were to lose a challenge to the law on First Amendment grounds, then for the whole summer ahead (until the legislature was back in session to repair it) the state, and the public-at-large, would be facing a host of unregulated commercial events whose profit-driven promoters could get away with inadequate sanitation, unpotable water, unsafe ingress and egress, insufficient medical backup, no insurance and any number of other conceivable real problems.

Now how did the State of North Carolina get itself into this jam with the Rainbow Family? Not just because the Rainbows selected the beautiful Smoky Mountain Region to hold their annual get-together. No, it took some cajoling on the part of the United States

Forest Service.

In 1984, some three years earlier, the Forest Service enacted a regulation aimed specifically at these Rainbow Events. How do we know it was aimed at these Rainbow Events? Well, for one thing, it was on the Forest Service books for a year-and-a-half before any Ranger went to enforce it on anyone – and it demanded a permit for any expressive assembly of ten or more people anywhere on U.S. Forest lands. Surely in a year-and-a-half there were thousands of expressive meetings – prayer groups, environmental assemblies, scholar's discussions, poet's readings, etc., etc. – out in our National Forests. Then all of a sudden anytime there's a Rainbow Gathering, here come the Rangers, and their enforcement agents demanding that the group select a representative to sign their paperwork.

The Rainbows, myself among them, went to trial in Tucson, Arizona in the spring of 1986.

Judge Bilby presided. He asked the prosecutor, "Do you mean to tell me that if I were out in the public forests with nine Lutheran Ministers discussing the Bible, and a tenth Minister showed up, that we would be required to stop our discussion and go and get ourselves a permit or else we'd be in violation of the law?"

"Well, um, er, no, Your Honor, I don't think that you'd --"

"But these Rainbows? You'd require them to go and get themselves a permit. Isn't that the case?" Judge Bilby interrupted him.

So Judge Bilby found that the Forest Service regulation was "impermissibly" unconstitutional, in part because it required expressive events to obtain permission while non-expressive events were not so required.

This rankled the Forest Service. To have lost a constitutional case to this bunch of hippies! The bureaucrats in Washington went on trying to figure out how to write a law that would allow them to regulate these free-form, free-thinking, free-acting citizens, but by the time the North Carolina Gathering of 1987 came around they hadn't figured out how to do so.

So instead they approached the well-meaning officers of the State of North Carolina with a stern warning about these nekkid hippies, these unkempt vagabonds who were going to descend like locusts upon their dear forests, and there just wasn't a thing their Rangers could do about it ... unless the State, the good State of North Carolina came to their aid.

I don't know if it was Lacy Thornburg, the State's Attorney General, they first approached, or if it was Ron Levine, the State Health Supervisor, but I heard many times over that the nudge to act came from the Forest Service. And so, act they did. First, people in the field were actively scouting, then following the leads of the various pamphlets and flyers back to the post office boxes they were mailed from, and then lawfully uncovering who were the keyholders of those Post Office boxes, and then, wham, slapping them by name with a suit commanding them to comply with the aforementioned Mass Gathering Act.

I was one of those keyholders to one of those boxes, from so long ago that I hadn't actually held the key in my own hand for years. Still before I'd even set foot – or set the wheel of my schoolbus – onto the soil of North Carolina, there I was, named in the suit.

Obviously we were sent to State Court, and on the wise advice of our ACLU-trained lawyer, Mike, we transferred as swiftly as we could – on account of diversity of citizenship – into Federal procedures, and that, that is how we landed before Judge Dave.

And here you have the essence of the conundrum: Now the Rainbows, who by experience know a bit about fighting unconstitutional laws, are embroiled in a lawsuit under a law that cannot lawfully demand such numerous restrictions of non-commercial users. How do you settle the case without abolishing a law which has important purposes for commercial types of mass assemblies, without dismissing the fair concerns of the commonwealth toward the health and safety of the public, and without beheading the rights of peaceful assembly that we all really value?

Judge Dave solved the puzzle by cracking the nutshell without cracking the nut. Ultimately, he ordered both sides to come to terms with the genuine issues of concern, without invoking the inapplicable Mass Gathering law. Does it have to take a Solomon or a Socrates or a Solon to see through these mysteries? No, it just took a good man with an open mind and common sense.

2 ✦ A FEW WORDS ABOUT MYSELF

When, during his narrative, Judge Dave muses trepidatiously about what I do for income, and Mr. Cansler is bold enough to ask, they both remain uncertain about the meaning of the answer my friends give them: "He's a consultant." To clear this up: I worked, at that time, for the Mid-Atlantic Office of the Trust for Public Land, technically as a "consultant." But my daily work was as Project Designer and co-ordinator for their New York City Children's Gardening Program.

We took schoolchildren from the city's public schools, daycare centers, private schools, religious schools and turned vacant lots or cement-covered yards into community gardens.

Ultimately we were teaching the real science of the lifecycle of plants, and the students were getting higher science test scores and the neighborhoods were getting beautiful public greenspaces. I helped write the program's textbook – really a teacher's curriculum guide – that is still in print, and is also today finding some interest among home-schooling advocates. We developed a "mentor" program, where middle school and high school students, some of whom were "graduates" of our Garden Program themselves, would help teach the younger children's classes. The program grew to include thousands of schoolchildren in dozens of community gardens. Most of those gardens are still there, as part of New York City's permanent greenspace. I did this for nine years between 1984 and 1993. It was the best, most rewarding work I ever had.

Judge Dave also has me described as a "storyteller" – at least semi-professionally. And indeed that was and still is the case. I do practice what I think is the art of storytelling and I've been fortunate to have had audiences to spin tales to at campfires in the woods, at renaissance faires in the countryside, at spoken word events and art fairs in big cities, with Garrison Keillor on his Prairie Home Companion, with Bob Fass on New York's WBAI, and, of course, on rustic stages at many, many Rainbow Gatherings.

But it's no easy thing to get paid work as a "storyteller." And even when you do, it's a small sum, a sort of thank you. It's not a big-paying art form.

And at the point in his narrative where I am pulled by a couple of young Rainbows away from the Judge's tour – on what seemed to him (and to me!) to be some kind of pretense concerning storytelling – in fact the situation was this: My son had his first bee sting right by Kiddie Village and was undergoing a severe allergic reaction. The attending physicians and his mother sent a couple of young messenger runners to find me, telling them to look for a group that was off in a particular direction, and that would appear to have several mainstream-dressed types, accompanied by Rainbow types, taking a "tour" of the camp. So these young people found me, and delivered the "important" message urging me away from the tour, without disrupting the procession and without panicking me. Only when we were alone along the trail did they tell me that I was being called to a family medical emergency. Luckily, by the time I arrived at Kiddie Village, an "eppie shot" had been administered and my boy was slowly recovering.

3 ✤ ONE RALPH, TWO RALPHS, RUSSIAN BOARS & RUMORS GALORE

As I read Judge Dave's account, it's clear that he really grasps the truly non-organized, independent nature of the people's participation in the processes of the event. There has been so much press over decades that doesn't look beyond the pagentry, the drumming, the colorful fashions, the common acceptance of nakedness, the parades, and so forth. And very little has been recorded about the massive and complex volunteer participation that maintains our woodland village.

Equal to the Judge's view of the colorful angle is the Judge's understanding and observance of how all this runs on people's independently motivated hard work.

It's a lot of work to dig all those latrines. It's a lot of work to park all those cars and buses so well, to maintain all those shuttles, to truck in, distribute, and cook all the food, and to clean up and recycle all the trash. The gatherings run on the feet of many people.

Alongside all the descriptions of the Judge's meetings with the quirky Rainbows, we can read his observations of the water, food, transportation, waste disposal, medical, and childcare systems that are the underpinnings of any functional society. And they are here, just as they must be in any village or metropolis.

Two vehicles really could pass safely on the roadway up the hill. But for the most part everyone operated with a radio and baton-pass communications system to keep either uphill or downhill traffic going at any one time. The road was winding, and there were enough larger rigs and drivers without much forest road experience to justify using a one-way-at-a-time system for safety's sake.

On tour, to be fair, we brought the Judge to the two different latrine sites simply because one was by a smaller neighborhood, and the other was a facility just off the Main Meadow and was used by way many more people. We thought it was important to show both.

You can see the info center he writes about on the far side of the July 4th picture at the end of these reflections.

I think there is more than one "Ralph" in the Judge's

story. The oufit he's described as wearing isn't that uncommon, and I think our narrator may have merged a couple of these characters in his memory. Still, the instances he relates of "Ralph's" actions – at least the ones I was present for – are all accurate.

As to the Russian Boars. The Wild Hog Theory of how we contracted shigellosis was then just one of many theories that both we and the CDC considered. Ultimately, the CDC indicated that the strain was not a match for any of the several hundred strains previously tested here in the United States. They concluded that the strain was most likely brought into the encampment by a carrier who had traveled recently in Asia.

There were a lot of other theories: There had been a small camp briefly above one of the springs; The Forest Service was trying to poison us; Some weirdo had poured it in the water supply; People swore they saw a cropduster dispense reddish clouds over the camp; Wild hogs roamed the woods and wallowed in the marshy spring pools. It was hard to know what to believe. But it was a mean stomach parasite. We read the CDC materials carefully. From that lesson, whatever the source, the Gatherings have grown much more aware about hand-washing both personally, and especially for food preparers and food servers.

4 ✦ OUR DAYS IN COURT

A few words of homage ought be paid here to the two gentlemen who testified about the ecology of the site's water resources, both of whom Judge Dave aptly characterizes as reliable witnesses, and both of whom have recently passed from this earth.

The first, the biologist known as Sunbear to the Rainbows, who spoke about the details of the Gathering's composting systems, solar hot water showers, grey water disposal systems, solid waste recycling, spring water outputs, and distances of kitchens and privies from springs and streams, was eager to volunteer to testify. He had been involved in the set-up of many of these systems, had two relevant college degrees, and was well aware of the brewing court hearing.

Despite Sunbear's credentials, our lawyer Mike insisted that, in the face of the State's impending testimony about the perilous nature of the proximity of the gathering to the public reservoir, we needed more than one witness to the efficacy of the Gathering's systems. We needed someone who could testify about the geology of the region. "Get me somebody with a degree!" he implored. "There's 17,000 people up there. Someone's got to have some letters after their name. A geology degree, a soil scientist, a water hydraulicist, somebody who can make the case that you're not going to pollute the town's water supply. That's what I need! That's what you need."

So we drove the three hours back to the camp. Parked. Hiked across the blockaded bridge. Shuttled up the hill. It was dark. It was late. Everyone wanted to talk about everything, and all I was trying to do was to locate our needed Scientist. We sent runners out to every camp that had late-night events. Announcements were made from the Gypsy Theatre Stage, and during the lulls at the thunderous drum circle. Runners came back shrugging their shoulders, without results, and without much hope.

I persuaded my good friend Joseph that this particular quest was crucial and he relentlessly scoured the miles of trails seaching among the remaining awake campfire circles. As the night grew long, he returned breathlessly up from the steep hill that led to the sweat lodges. "I think I've found him. But he's gone into the sweat lodge and won't be out for an hour or maybe more." It was already 4 a.m. and we'd have to leave by 5:30 just to be at the courtroom on time. So Joseph waited at the door to the sweat lodge and, as the participants in the ceremony emerged, he corraled Gill (Dr. William Smith to the Court) and led him to us at the Bus Village.

Gill was naked except for the towel slung over his shoulder. He had a "pair" of glasses with only one eyeframe, hung on by only one earhook. His clothes were a mile and a half in the other direction and, glistening from the energy of the sweat, he was ready to go. "Can't I just testify in my towel?" he asked. "That would be decent enough for the court, wouldn't it? Is there some law about having to be well dressed in order to be believed?"

I was not so sure he was the ideal witness, but we rounded him up some clothes, wired his other eyeglass half together, and stuffed him and his lovely girlfriend – who was quite upset about not being able to wander with him through the woods back to their tent together – into our car, and off we went to the halls of justice and the courtroom of Judge Dave.

En route we found out what a truly excellent witness we had indeed. B.A. in Geology, B.S. in Environmental Sciences, Ph.D. in Geology. He'd been onsite for a month, scouted out the springs, selected kitchen locations, and had already familiarized himself with the underlying geology of the region's mountains. He was a veritable encyclopedia of knowledge about the particulars of waterflow. He directed Peace Corps projects for village water development, worked in the U.S. Navy with water resources in remote areas, and he modestly admitted to having helped (in a junior capacity) during his Ph.D. studies on a research project that won its author a Nobel Prize. By the time we had him dressed in a conservative flannel shirt and clean jeans and had brushed his hair, he was ready ... and standing before the maps Judge Dave requisitioned from the State's library, he was holding the pointer, lecturing all of us, including the State's Watermaster about the "impermeable" layer that separates the Gathering area from the Cheoha Reservoir and about seepage rates through various geological formations. It was a nice moment.

Gill passed away a few years ago in New York City, and Sunbear, one of the "bankers" helping with the "magic hat" at the 1999 Gathering in Pennsylvania, collapsed of heart failure onsite at the tail end of that event. His ashes were spread ceremoniously at the New England regional Gathering in the White Mountains later that same year. They were kind and devoted "brothers" and they had their day in court.

Just as Judge Dave relates, later that afternoon we hammered out, paragraph by paragraph, the consent agreement he ordained. And then we once more rode back to camp, and spent a long hard day trying to convince the council that this was a good solution to a knotty problem. But the council wasn't going to consense to Stephen and me signing anything on behalf of all the free-thinking free spirits gathering freely in those free mountains.

So the following day, when we returned to Judge Dave's Federal Courthouse, we ourselves were uncertain how things would turn out. But in an odd, and untasteful, twist of events the State of North Carolina made matters both worse and better at the same time.

The document we had left the Judge's chambers with

had exactly twenty-two paragraphs. Each one carefully tailored to a specific "need" of the State, and each one written to balance with the undeniable "rights" of assembly of the Rainbows. But when we returned to the Judge's courtroom, a remarkable new paragraph "number twenty-one" had been added, bring the total paragraphs now up to twenty-three.

And what did this new un-discussed paragraph add? It added that if, in the State's view, any of the other paragraphs weren't perfectly met, the original lawsuit against us wouldn't be dropped and the named defendants would be liable to renewed charges! On the way into the courtroom all the lawyers' buzz was: don't try to change anything. Don't stall, don't add, don't object, don't complain. Just say "Yes," and sign.

And there we were, reading the document with this new paragraph added. And after, "All Rise!" Judge Dave asked if anyone else had anything to say, and all the lawyers said, "No, Your Honor." My co-defendant Stephen raised his hand, the Judge recognized him, and Stephen boldly spoke up about this new, un-discussed paragraph being added behind everyone's back – including the Judge's – and Stephen suggested that the only way – the *only* way – this document could be signed was "Under Duress!"

The prosecutor slammed his hand down onto his table, our lawyer Mike flicked his pencil up end over end into the air, as if to say, "Well, there goes the ball game!" And Judge Dave in a swift and succinctly brilliant decision said that he would accept that. And so Stephen read into the record, and submitted as a formal addition to the case's paperwork, a statement that the document as given over was being signed "under a sense of duress" and that paragraph twenty-one had been "inserted by [the] State in Bad Faith."

The prosecutor continued to object and we were all summoned to the Judge's bench, where he explained that This Was The Way It Was Going To Be. At that time I was able briefly to explain that our council had consensed that Stephen and I were not given the okay to sign anything, but that another equally reasonable Rainbow had volunteered to come forward and provide the necessary signature. So it was that actually Stephen and I did not sign the Consent Judgment, but another Rainbow, acceptable to both the Court and the State of North Carolina, did so.

And that was what happened. This signing part is the only inaccuracy in the whole of the Judge's account. Our names were typed onto the paperwork as planned, but the actual signature – and hand printed name and handwritten address – is someone else's.

5 ✳ *VIDEO VILLAINY?*

Pretty much, everyone kept to the terms of the Consent Agreement. Enough so that the Court and the State

both agreed in the end that its terms had been met, but along the way, video cameras entered the controversy.

The Forest Service began video recording every license plate of every vehicle attending the event. They ran their own vehicles slowly along the lines of parked cars aiming their camera at the license tags. They did this day after day, and this aroused tremendous resentment and fear among people attending the gathering. This was not the same as recording the environmental situations or recording an overview of the happenings for future study and preparedness for public agencies better to be able to understand and deal with events like these.

No, I believed then, and I still believe, that this has what in First Amendment parlance is known as a "chilling effect" on expression. What cause does the government of any State whether it's Commie China or North Carolina have to make record of the tags of all the attendees at an expressive assembly? What right do they have to concoct such a list?

What if some government agency had chosen to videotape all the license plate numbers at the parking lot each Sunday at the Baptist Church where good Judge Dave teaches his adult Gospel lessons?? What if that? Then maybe Judge Dave might not take such a mild view of this kind of activity.

That's what led to people holding up their hands in front of the cameras as the Forest Service Law Enforcement paraded them about the encampment. And when one officer moved forward and touched his camera lens to the hand of a non-violent protester, that's what lead to the arrest on the road a day later that the Judge chronicles in his telling.

It was these kind of abuses of enforcement powers that gave rise to everyone's call for additional oversight by the good Judge's court.

Another example. At the tail end of the Gathering, thousands, and then hundreds, and finally dozens of volunteers worked so hard, using just hand tools, to aerate soil, disappear all traces of the encampment, vanish trails, insert waterbars, bury compost and remove trash. In the end only a couple of dozen hardworking volunteers remained, and only a couple of large trash piles stood next to the final "cleanup camp."

There wasn't a great deal of work left to be done. Maybe another two days, and that would be it. All done. Cleaned up and gone quietly. But the U.S. Forest Service ordered the Forest "Closed" and ordered everyone to leave the site. The cleanup crew that remained objected, saying that the job was almost entirely done, and they weren't going until it was fully completed. But the Forest "Law" officers insisted upon their order, and then arrested six members of the cleanup crew who wouldn't leave the job undone.

And then what did the Forest Service do? They brought in their video camera and photgraphed the two remaining piles of trash. They videoed them from every possible angle, and put these into a Forest Service training film about Rainbow events, purporting to show how the Rainbows leave piles of trash behind them wherever they go. Video villainy? You be the judge.

The Forest Service presented these tainted videos in Federal Court the following year in Texas. The Court discounted their allegations, specifically referring to the U.S. Forest Service actions in 1987 in North Carolina. The Court noted, "Indeed, there is substantial support for the defendants' argument that the government has acted with hostility to the Rainbow Family."

6 ✤ *IN THE JUDGE'S CHAMBERS*

What with so many people coming down with intestinal troubles, and the local folks pointing out the wild garlic that grew on the hillsides as a cure for most local ailments, I dunno, maybe somebody was eating ramps.

In any case, the Marshal's careful explanation to me about prejudice and policing has stayed with me to this day. I may not have wanted to hear what I heard, but hear it I did, and his rendition of the forces that shape the world we are in gave me a broader understanding of how we sometimes have to accept what we don't want in order to live within the world as it really is.

7 ❧ AND IN THE END

As I look back over the events of that summer's Gathering, I remember most of all, the big grand quietness of all those people sitting in that huge meadow in deep real silence, in the Meditation for Peace.

Despite all the hullabaloo, and all the commotion both before and afterwards, there was a time, between the break of dawn and high noon, when it seemed the world stood quietly still, and the wind blew through our hair, the tree limbs swayed just slightly as they do when only an occasional breeze rustles through them, and the clouds moved serenely across the Smoky Mountains' sunlit sky. And in those hours and moments I was able to give thanks. And I had so much to be thankful for. For the Earth, the Sky, the Water. For my children, and all the beautiful children, the inheritors of all the hope.

Garrick Beck

March 3RD, 2002

 HAPPY TRAILS!

David B. Sentelle graduated with honors in 1968 from the University of North Carolina Law School. He was an associate with the firm of Uzzell & Dumont, in Asheville, North Carolina, and then served as Assistant United States Attorney in Charlotte, North Carolina. From 1974 to 1977, he was a North Carolina State District Judge in Charlotte. He then became a partner of Tucker, Hicks, Sentelle, Moon & Hodge. In the fall of 1985, he was appointed to the U.S. District Court for the Western District of North Carolina, where he served until his appointment on October 19, 1987 to the U.S. Court of Appeals for the D.C. Circuit.

Judge Sentelle serves as presiding judge of the Special Division of the Court for the Appointment of Independent Counsels. He is also President of the Edward Bennett Williams Inn of the American Inns of Court, a member of the Edward Coke Appellate Inn of Court, and a member of the Board of the American Inns of Court Foundation.